The Gift of Intensity

Also by Imi Lo

Emotional Sensitivity and Intensity

The Gift of Intensity

*How to Win at Life and Love as a Highly
Sensitive and Emotionally Intense Person*

IMI LO

JOHN
MURRAY
LEARNING

First published in Great Britain by John Murray Learning in 2021
An imprint of John Murray Press
A division of Hodder & Stoughton Ltd,
An Hachette UK company

This paperback edition published in 2023

1

A CIP catalogue record for this title is available from the British Library

Paperback ISBN 978 1 529 34116 4
eBook ISBN 978 1 529 34117 1

Typeset by KnowledgeWorks Global Ltd.

Printed and bound in Great Britain by Clays Ltd, Elcograf S.p.A.

John Murray Press policy is to use papers that are natural, renewable and recyclable
products and made from wood grown in sustainable forests. The logging and
manufacturing processes are expected to conform to the environmental regulations of
the country of origin.

John Murray Press
Carmelite House
50 Victoria Embankment
London EC4Y 0DZ

www.johnmurraypress.co.uk

Contents

Introduction

This book is written for those among us who are exceptionally intense, sensitive and empathic in nature. This book is for you if you have never fitted in with the mainstream, and have no choice but to walk an unconventional path.

All your life, you have been told you are 'too much', 'too strange', 'too difficult' or 'too dramatic'. You are a deep thinker, an intuitive feeler and an extraordinary observer. When you see pain in others, you feel it in your heart. When art or music moves you, you are flooded with waves of joy and ecstasy. As a natural empathizer, you have a gift; you see social nuances and emotional dynamics that are missed by most people, and you also absorb psychic energy from those around you.

As a child, you were spirited, perceptive and sensitive. You had insatiable curiosity and a rich inner world. You did not always agree with the adults in your life, and always challenged what was unjust and unfair. You were obsessed with certain subjects, and formed strong attachments to people, animals, objects and places.

Your passionate nature, intuition and independent think-ing set you apart from the mainstream, and being out-of-sync means your search for belongingness remains a perennial strug-gle. Sometimes, it seems your tribe or soulmate is nowhere to be found. Few can keep up with your intellect, and those who do may not share your emotional depth.

What works for others does not work for you. No matter how much you try, you cannot hold down a conventional job, climb the corporate ladder or walk the stable and predictable path. You are interested in too many things to be boxed into one stereotype or career. You have difficulties saying yes to hypocritical and dysfunctional systems, and find it hard to not be the whistleblower to the truth you see. Your family and friends say you are overly serious.

At some point in your life, after many rejections and criticisms, you took an unconscious vow to hide your true self so that you would never be hurt, rejected or betrayed again. You developed an adaptive social facade that is carefully edited, partially silenced and rigidly held. You made yourself invisible to curtail the disapproving gazes, the teasing, shaming and mocking. You moulded yourself into a more socially acceptable version, and 'mellowed out' your intensities in order to fit in.

Investing in a facade can take many forms. You may be stuck in an unsatisfactory job or a dysfunctional relationship, or perhaps you hold back from creative expression. Sometimes, you overstay in a community even when you clearly don't fit in, believing that if you try hard enough, you will find love and acceptance. After a while, you forgot your true nature – you forgot the spontaneous wild soul that you are. Though on the outside you appear secure, inwardly you feel numb and insecure. You have curbed your excitement, denied your longings and discarded your big dreams, and you have ended up with a limited palette for life.

Your false facade might have worked for a while, but your soul refuses to be banished. Your existential angst might have started with an illness, a relationship breakdown or a career crisis. Suddenly, you can no longer withstand hiding who you are, or the emptiness that comes from a lifetime of denial. You realize your authentic being is much more valuable than fusion with the masses. When life wakes you up, however turbulent the journey of reclaiming your true self might be, you have no choice but to embark upon it. Perhaps right now, you are at this critical juncture of your life.

> For a long time, you have thought there was something wrong with you. Never had you considered the possibility that your intensity is a sign of enormous creative potential.

This book tells a different story and will help you to re-define yourself. Here is an invitation for the return of your true nature.

Through the chapters in this book, you will learn to see the differences between true belongingness and false belongingness, how to heal from what has shamed and hurt you in the past, and ways to not just survive, but to thrive as an intense person. Instead of the roller coaster ride of social anxiety, and fear of rejection, you will learn to find peace in yourself.

If you have read my first book, *Emotional Sensitivity and Intensity*, you may already be familiar with some of the concepts found in *The Gift of Intensity*. This book hones in on the theme of 'relationships' to explore what it means to be an intense, non-conforming and sensitive person in this world.

Part 1 of this book sets out the premise, in which we review what it means to be intense and different. In Part 2 you will find strategies, exercises and advice that will help you thrive in relationships with yourself and others. This section is organized by the four relational circles in life:

In Chapter 4 'Your relationship with yourself', you will learn to develop emotional skills that help you navigate your complex and intense emotional landscape, as well as help you understand the value of reclaiming your true self as an intense person.

In Chapter 5 'Your relationship with your family', we will focus on your relationship with your family of origin. Being an apple that has fallen far from the tree can hurt in ways that are invisible. We will examine some of the toxic family dynamics that may have wounded you deeply, the idea of forgiveness and what you can do to release burdens that have weighed you down.

In Chapter 6 'Romantic and intimate relationships', we will think about the challenges you face in intimate relationships. For example, you may have big ups and downs with your partners, be bored and restless, face frequent emotional triggers, and have difficulty when trying to control your reactions. Drawing from attachment and psychodynamic theories, you will learn how to undo the unhealthy patterns that hold you back from intimacy.

Finally, in Chapter 7 'Work relationships and friendships', we will consider your relationship with the wider social world – this includes people at work and friends. We help you to navigate common challenges at work, from power struggles to interpersonal dynamics. The section entitled 'Growing out of people' addresses a common but largely unnamed challenge faced by intense people: the tendency to grow out of people and the need to move on from relationships.

Ultimately, finding true belongingness in the world starts from embracing the fullness of who you are.

The most threatening thing in life is not that others reject you, but that you desert yourself. No matter what others think of you, or what happens in this wild and precarious world, you must have your own back. Once you have found 'home' within yourself, you will be capable of building healthy and fulfilling relationships with others. You will know where your boundaries are, who to invite into your world and who to keep out, how to manage your energies, and where to go to seek the love and recognition you deserve. At the end of this journey, you will no longer tolerate anything or anyone that does not honour your fullest potential as an intense and sensitive person.

You are more ready than you think you are. I look forward to being with you on the path from hiding to thriving!

Imi Lo

PART I

On being intense

I

Are you intense and sensitive?

Living with emotional intensity is a mixed blessing. At its best, your intensity feels like a quivering aliveness and gives you a deep appreciation for the world. At its worst, it feels like a consuming, out-of-control, never-ending storm inside you.

Being intense means that you are out-of-sync with those around you. Without guidance, you may not have learned how to appreciate your strengths and harness your gifts. Through learning about the intricacies of your intensity, I hope you can make sense of your life from a new perspective.

What is emotional intensity?

Emotional intensity comprises of the following five components:

1 Emotional depth and passion
2 Deep empathy and sensitivity
3 Being highly attuned and perceptive
4 A rich inner world, imbued with intellectual intensity and a vivid imagination
5 Creative potential and existential angst.

1 Emotional depth and passion

Whether or not you express them outwardly, you feel things deeply and intensely. Within the course of a single day, you may soar high into bliss then plunge deep into depression. You experience positive and negative feelings at the same time or in quick succession.

To you, feelings are not just feelings; they are a penetrative, absorbing, whole-body experience. Disappointment can be felt as despair, rage feels uncontainable, and you sometimes feel threatened by the strength of your feelings. Once you have learned how to manage it, however, your varied emotional landscape is what makes you exceptionally passionate and creative.

Small things in life can bring you ecstasy and rapture. When you immerse yourself in deep relationships, music, films and literature, it is difficult to pull yourself out of a transcendent state.

You feel the world at a wavelength that is not in sync with those around you. Compared to peers your age, you are an unusually deep thinker. You see the intricacy and complexity of human life and have always been an 'old soul'; at the same time, you have retained a child-like idealism and sense of wonder about the world.

You are extremely passionate and can become infatuated and obsessed with people and ideas. Even though you might not show it on the outside, you love fiercely and care deeply. This applies not only to romantic partners but also your friends, family, animals and the wider world.

You have a low tolerance for small talk and social niceties. You want to bypass the shallow interactions so you can build soulful and meaningful connections with others.

Your heart is naturally open, though through repeated rejections and your love not being reciprocated, you may have learned to close down and make yourself numb to protect yourself.

You form such strong connections with people, animals and places that separation is painful for you. You experience nostalgia frequently. When you recall a memory with someone you love, you feel and re-live it as though it was yesterday.

2 Deep empathy and sensitivity

You are hyper-empathic and 'absorb' other people's psychic and emotional materials. When you walk into a room, you cannot help but pick up on the nuanced emotions, unspoken social signals and other people's energies. This can make crowds or social situations overwhelming and exhausting.

From an early age, you have a deep concern for not just your immediate surroundings but also the welfare of the world. When you see other people and animals get hurt, you feel it as though it is happening to you.

You are sensitive to your friends' and lovers' needs. Being a loyal companion, you are there when they need you. Sometimes, you sense their sadness and frustration before they do.

You easily feel hurt by what other people say or don't say, do or don't do. People have commented that you have 'thin skin'. Sometimes you over-analyse interactions with others and, when conflict occurs, you are quick to assign blame to yourself.

You are easily overwhelmed by sensory input such as noises, strong smells or tactile sensations from clothing tags or rough surfaces. You may have misophonia (hatred of sound), hyper-acusis (sensitivity to sound), osmophobia (hypersensitivity to odour), hypergeusia (being a 'supertaster'), skin sensitivity and multiple allergies.

Your feelings are often somatized – manifested through physical symptoms. As a result of not being able to digest all that you have absorbed from the surroundings, you experience allergies, digestive issues, dysregulated heartbeat, chronic fatigue and frequent headaches.

3 Being highly attuned and perceptive

You see beyond the surface. For example, you see hypocrisies that others miss, and you can tell when someone is being incongruent. Even when someone does not admit they are upset, you can still sense their sadness.

You have a sense of knowing when something is about to happen, or about other people's inner worlds. Your intuition sometimes makes you feel like you are 'psychic'.

You are a keen observer of the world and are able to see situations from many perspectives. You see possibilities and alternatives to most situations.

When your perceptiveness is paired with a strong sense of justice, it can create interpersonal struggles for you. For example, you cannot help but challenge inequality and oppression at your workplace, or point out hypocrisies in your peer groups.

You are the whistleblower, or the one who reveals inconvenient truths, and people feel threatened by you because they feel you can see through them. You are the one who points out 'the elephant in the room' or tries to address the real issues that underlie the facade of normalcy.

You push the boundaries of conformity and question or challenge traditions, particularly those that seem meaningless or unethical. Although your path is not an easy one, your intuition and integrity can also make you a great visionary leader.

You are sensitive to the spiritual world or were drawn to spirituality from a young age. Even though you might not have a religious background, you feel connected to something in nature or something bigger than yourself.

4 A rich inner world imbued with intellectual intensity and vivid imagination

You are not only emotionally but also intellectually intense (the two often go together). You have a fast brain that processes information rapidly and can learn new things quickly. You have deep and complex thoughts, and you are highly capable of abstract reasoning.

Your mind runs on multiple tracks. You may have a constant stream of ideas, so many that you feel you cannot keep up with or execute them.

When you are excited, your mind runs too fast for your words; you find yourself talking rapidly, perhaps even interrupting others. You may appear critical and impatient with those who cannot keep up with you.

As a natural truth-seeker, you have a strong need to understand, to expand your horizons and to gain knowledge. You are likely an avid reader and a rigorous researcher. From a young age you have felt an urge to leave home to explore the world, though you may feel guilty for leaving people behind.

You have a rich inner world that consists of a vivid imagination, fantasies and dreams. You think not just in words, but also in images and metaphors.

When you become absorbed in a new project, an imaginative vision or when you are engaged with a piece of art, literature, theatre or music, the outside world ceases to exist for you.

If your childhood environment was chaotic, abusive or under-stimulating, you might have resorted to excessive daydreaming about your imagined world as a way to cope. Books, the arts, nature, imaginary friends or spirit animals became your safe haven in times of emotional turmoil.

You have a wide range of interests and feel frustrated in a world that wants you to specialize. Even though you might have chosen a conventional career path, you cannot curb your curiosity and passion for other disciplines.

5 Creative potential and existential angst

You look for meaning in life. From a young age, you experienced existential depression and thought about issues such as the meaninglessness of life, death and loneliness. You were frustrated that those around you, especially the adults, were not

7

prepared to discuss and consider these weighty concerns with you.

You are an autonomous worker and think independently. You do not take directions that don't make sense to you, and challenge authorities that are tyrannical. Your work is driven by an internal drive to learn and understand, rather than any extrinsic awards such as money or fame.

Being able to see the deepest potential of things also means you are painfully aware of how the current situation falls short of the ideal. You feel overwhelmingly sad by the state of the world, and the injustice, inequality and oppression that exists.

For unknown reasons, you feel a weight of responsibility on your shoulders – even for things you are not responsible for. You may be haunted by a sense of urgency, a constant impulse to move forward. You get a constant 'niggling' feeling that there is something important for you to achieve. You live with a feeling that somehow time is running out, and you are not doing what you should be doing.

You bring a high level of integrity to your work and have high standards for both yourself and others. What seems normal to you can seem 'perfectionist' and demanding to others.

You are highly inquisitive and diligently reflect on your behaviour. The flip side is that you are occupied with obsessive thoughts and scrupulous self-examination.

When you have a strong vision or innovative idea, you feel the split between belongingness and authentic expression – you want to express with your full, authentic self but you are worried that it will result in being rejected.

When your idealism becomes perfectionism, it paralyses you. You may be prone to creative blockages such as 'artist's block', 'writer's block', procrastination, the fear of exposure or Imposter Syndrome (the feeling that you are a fraud).

Seeing yourself clearly and accurately will help you to reframe the meaning of your struggles. Rather than wishing you were someone else, you will come to embrace your unique life path. In this process, you will realize that the most profound pain comes not from being outside of the herd, but from disowning your true self. If you can embrace it, you will come to see your intensity as your most profound gift.

2
Being intense is a brain difference

Through advancement in neuroscience, psychologists are beginning to see 'neurodiversity' — the fact that we are all wired differently — as something to be celebrated. Rather than eliminating what does not seem to fit into the 'norm', we can observe the many ways we flourish as human beings.

We are each born with a unique temperament; it comprises of individual differences that are:

- Biologically based
- Evident early in life
- Remain constant characteristics in many situations over time.

> Emotional intensity, high sensitivity and the tendency to be hyper-empathic are overlapping traits that constitute the temperament of a highly intense person.

These are brain differences that follow you from the get-go. In this chapter, we draw upon existing concepts, research and psychological theories to understand the origins of these traits, the gifts they indicate and how you can harness these strengths.

Some of us are born sensitive

From birth, we differ from each other in the ways we react to external stimuli and sensations.[1] Jerome Kagan, a Harvard developmental psychologist, was one of the first people to study sensitivity as a brain difference. In his study, he found that some babies were more reactive to stimulations such as a strong smell and loud noises; they also tended to be more distressed by the intrusion of strangers. These infants' reactions had a biochemical basis: their brain secreted a higher level of norepinephrine (the brain's version of adrenaline) and stress hormones such as cortisol.[2] They were more primed towards detecting threats and, although in a way this is an evolutionary advantage, they were also quick to react to benign stressors. Even as adults, sensitive individuals are more vulnerable to accumulating stress in their bodies, resulting in physical ailments such as chronic pain, fatigue, allergies and migraine headaches.

Highly sensitive people

In 1995, Elaine Aron (2013) published the book *The Highly Sensitive Person* (HSP), bringing the concept into the mainstream.[3] Aron suggests 15–20 per cent of the population are highly sensitive and it is just as common among men as among women. Compared to the average population, HSPs have a more reactive immune system and nervous system. This means they experience physiological as well as psychological reactions to stimuli such as crowded spaces, strong odours, rough surfaces and loud noises. Like their adult counterparts, highly sensitive children are easily overwhelmed by sudden changes; they also tend to feel and absorb the emotional distress of others. However, depending on the temperamental fit with their parents, how they come across varies – some are labelled as 'weird', 'sensitive' or 'shy', others as 'difficult', 'active', 'demanding' and 'stubborn'.

Here are some of the HSP traits drawn from the self-test designed by Aron (2019):[4]

- Startling easily
- Being very sensitive to pain

- Getting rattled when you have a lot to do in a short amount of time
- Enjoying delicate or fine scents, tastes, sounds or works of art
- Getting easily overwhelmed by things such as bright lights, strong smells, coarse fabrics or nearby sirens
- Needing to avoid violent scenes in movies or TV shows
- Needing to withdraw to bed or a darkened room on busy days, gaining relief from privacy.

The concept of the HSP does not fully capture all dimensions of the intense personality as laid out in this book. While there are significant overlaps between the two, the dimensions of rigour, speed, passion and excitability can be added to the description of an intense person. In the original HSP concept, sensitive individuals are described as those who are startled and rattled easily. It is said that change can shake up the HSP, and competition can lead to nervousness or shakiness (except for a small sub-group of 'sensation-seeking' HSPs who seek out novelty and risk). In general, they are advised to arrange their life to avoid upsetting situations. Most HSP self-help books and therapists place great emphasis on limiting stimulations[5] and avoiding becoming overwhelmed. If you are not only sensitive but also intense, however, this advice is sufficient. For you, being under-stimulated is as problematic as being over-stimulated. Wellness does not mean becoming phobic of experiences, but rather finding a sweet spot where you attain adequate but not excessive challenges. To achieve a state of 'flow',[6] an adequate degree of vigour is needed in all aspects of your life, including work, love, relationships and daily activities. For instance, you can be dissatisfied in a relationship that under-stimulates you, or get burned out at work with too much mundane work where the tasks are intellectually too easy for you. In these scenarios, challenges, competitions and being in the spotlight can help. Staying well as an intense person is a balancing act – your goal is to find the right dose of intellectual, emotional and physical challenges, rather than bubble-wrapping yourself and taking a smaller and smaller slice of life.

Orchids and dandelions

Given society's entrenched stigma about emotional sensitivity, you may ask: is being born sensitive a disadvantage? Does it destine a person to a life of difficulties? In an attempt to answer these questions, Thomas Boyce came up with the 'Orchid and Dandelion' theory.[7]

Boyce and his team studied children and observed their developments in the long term. Through their research, Boyce found that 80 per cent of the population are relatively insensitive; just like dandelions in the wild, they survive most circumstances. The rest, the 20 per cent, are like orchids – exquisitely sensitive to their environment and vulnerable in adversity. The 80/20 split in their findings roughly parallels Aron's research into highly sensitive people. The 'Orchid and Dandelion' theory explains why siblings brought up in the same family might respond differently to dysfunctional family dynamics or parental distress. While no amount of childhood abuse or neglect is too little, Orchid children detect and are impacted by even the most subtle differences in their parents' feelings and behaviours, while Dandelion children remain unperturbed in comparison.

The most hope-giving aspect of the Orchid and Dandelion research lies in the result of their longitudinal studies, where they observe a group of people for a number of years. It turns out that, although sensitive children are more affected by adverse scenarios, they are also more receptive to favourable conditions. When given the right amount of support, they are more likely to flourish and prosper than their less sensitive counterparts. Many of Boyce's Orchid child patients have grown up to become eminent adults, magnificent parents, intelligent and generous citizens of the world. In other words, sensitivity is not inherently bad, but more like a 'highly leveraged evolutionary bet' that carries both high risks and high potential rewards.[8]

Are you an empath?

The word 'empath' has become increasingly common in recent years. Online articles and self-help books have been written about this special population who possess a higher than normal level of empathy. It is said that empaths have the gift of detecting others' feelings, but they can also become an 'emotional sponge' for others' energies. Here are some of the traits of an 'empath' according to Judith Orloff:[9]

- Naturally giving, spiritually open and good listeners
- Easily hurt in relationships
- Highly attuned to others' moods and tend to absorb other people's emotions
- Easy targets for 'energy vampires'
- Mostly introverted and needs alone time
- Highly attuned senses – can feel frayed by noises, smells or excessive talking
- Big hearts – often give too much to the point of burning out.

Despite mounting attention to the concept, the word 'empath' is misleading. Although it is true that some people are more empathic than others, we are all capable of empathy. It is more accurate to use the term 'hyper-empathy' to describe the tendency to be emotionally and energetically hyper-attuned. Hyper-empathic people are acutely aware, not just physically, but also psychically and socially. When they walk into a room, they detect the nuance, subtexts and energy flows. Without any conscious awareness, they are 'downloading' other people's psychic materials into their bodies. This ability can seem mystical, but on closer examination, theories in psychology can help us understand it. For instance, the research on emotional contagion and mirror neurons may shed some light on the science behind hyper-empathic abilities.

Being prone to emotional contagion

Social psychologists have long been interested in the idea of people 'catching' others' feelings, and they named this phenomenon 'emotional contagion'. Many studies have supported the idea that, as social beings, we unconsciously mimic the emotional expressions of others, to the point of actually feeling the same thing.[10]

With regards to the 'empath' phenomenon, the question is: are some people more susceptible to catching other people's feelings? According to social science research, the answer is yes.[11] In any interaction between two or more people, there will be one party with a more forceful emotional orbit, who can more powerfully infect others with their feelings. These are the emotional 'senders'. On the other hand, some people are more easily infected with others' emotions and are known as the 'catchers'. Each person's brain-wiring and personality factors determines who plays the senders and who plays the catchers. Senders tend to be more charismatic, expressive, entertaining, and scoring high on dominance as a trait,[12] while catchers are usually those who are attentive to the emotional details in their surroundings.

However, just automatically picking up on what others feel does not make a person empathic. Emotional contagion is a rapid, unconscious and automatic process, and it is not always productive. Emotional contagion is primitive, automatic and uncontrollable. It happens before we know it; we may pick up on others' psychic materials but fail to digest, transform or make use of them. Empathy, on the other hand, is a sophisticated cognitive process that takes more work.[13] If, as a hyper-empathic person, you only have unregulated emotion contagion, and all you do is sponge up other people's feelings, you can quickly become overwhelmed. To be effectively and healthily empathic, you need to develop skills such as context observation and emotional regulation so you can move beyond emotional contagion. Empathy requires a degree of emotional roundness, maturity and practice. It is a skill that can be learned, but once honed, it becomes the foundation of social intelligence, happiness and gifted leadership.

Having highly active mirror neurons

Apart from the social science perspective, neuroscience also contributes to our understanding of hyper-empathic tendencies. In recent years, scientists have discovered a set of neurons in our brain, known as mirror neurons. These cells create a neuro-physical link between us and other people, so that when we observe someone else doing something, the same regions in our brain, which would have been involved had we been doing it, become activated. In the same way, just seeing another person's emotions automatically creates an automatic resonance in our bodies and mind.[14] Scientists refer to this phenomenon as 'neural resonance' or 'brain-to-brain coupling'.[15] The work of mirror neurons is powerful because it generates a direct and neurological link between people, bypassing cognitive reasoning. Mirroring is a core facet of parenting, psychotherapy and other processes that require deep empathy. Our mirror neuron system can be over- or under-active, depending on many factors. Neuropsychological findings have confirmed that humans empathize with each other to different degrees,[16] and it is likely that people who are hyper-empathic have a more active mirror neuron system compared to the norm.

Being a childhood trauma survivor

Factors contributing to hyper-empathy can be both nature and nurture. If you are hyper-empathic, it is likely that by nature you have a sensitive physical and psychological system, permeable energy boundaries, and are more emotionally responsive to your surroundings. At the same time, certain childhood environments can amplify this trait. If you have grown up in a chaotic, violent or abusive childhood environment, becoming highly attuned might have been the only way you could survive. In environments that are unpredictable, the brain adapts by extracting patterns from information.[17] If you had to deal with highly unstable parents, you will have become extremely aware of the micro-changes in their energy levels, facial expressions and tone of voice. Inadvertently, you will have trained yourself to pick up on the earliest, most subtle signals of their outrage or attacks. When your empathic intuition is amplified by a precarious environment, you will experience hypervigilance and anxiety. Even, as a grown-up, when you are no longer facing any danger, whenever there are changes in the atmosphere of a room or the emotional tone of other people, you will still have an automatic and visceral fight-or-flight reaction, such as a tightening of the chest, increased heartbeat and a feeling that 'something ought to be done'.

Your energy boundaries can also be compromised if your caregivers in your childhood were excessively needy, controlling or engulfing. Parents who are emotionally immature or inadequate have a fear of not being needed or being abandoned by their children. They may – subtly, through outpouring emotions, guilt-tripping or manipulation – stop their child from separating from them. In psychoanalysis, the term 'ego boundary' is used to describe emotional and identity distinction between the self and others. If your parents repeatedly intruded in your space, you will not have had the opportunity to healthily individualize, and to separate your own psyche from others. You might be locked in a family dynamic called enmeshment – where two or more people are overly involved with and emotionally reactive to one another. In an enmeshed dynamic, a person is conditioned to be intensely affected by, and feel responsible for, other people's feelings. As a result, they struggle to tell the difference between their feelings and the feelings of those they are close to, and they may feel a constant compulsion to rescue others from their negative feelings. (These dynamics will be discussed further in Chapter 5.)

Overexcitabilities and giftedness

Unknown to most, intensity is a universal characteristic of gifted children and adults.[18] Your immediate reaction on seeing the word 'gifted' might be to cringe. It is a loaded term in our society and is misunderstood by many people. The traditional definition of 'giftedness' has been limited, often associated only with IQ or traditional talents such as music or sports. Nevertheless, there are infinite forms of extraordinary abilities not captured in the conventional conception. Alongside intellectual rigour, many intense people possess a high level of interpersonal intelligence – the ability to understand and relate wisely to others; intrapersonal intelligence – the capacity to reflect deeply and have accurate self-awareness; and existential intelligence – the ability to create meaning in life and tap into a sense of interconnectedness with other living and non-living beings.[19]

According to the 'hyper brain/hyper body theory',[20] people with high cognitive ability also have hyper-reactive physical symptoms, and their sympathetic nervous system may be chronically activated. Potentially, in such people, sensory information reaches the brain much faster than average, and the information is processed in a significantly shorter time. This results in heightened excitability in multiple dimensions, known as 'overexcitability'. This is a term translated from Polish *nadpobudliwość*. Since the phrase 'over' might give the wrong impression of meaning unnatural or undesirable, a better translation would be 'super-stimulatability'.[21] There are five forms of overexcitability: psychomotor, sensual, imaginational, intellectual and emotional. Each contributes to specific traits, strengths and qualities.[22]

Intellectual overexcitability

Intellectual overexcitability is a trait that drives you to constantly search for knowledge and truth. With it, your brain is always wanting to learn, problem-solve, analyse and reflect. You have a constant hunger to know more, and you feed that by reading, travelling and researching. You are intellectually precocious, immensely curious about the world and an astute observer. You are highly capable of reflective thinking and synthesizing complex theories. You are an independent and critical thinker, who does not accept things at face value. As a child, you often asked 'why?' and challenged the adults around you to think about issues they would not otherwise ponder, and you don't give up on a question until you find the answer.

When you get excited about an idea, you feel as though your brain will not stop; while your curiosity and drive feel normal to you, they seem obsessive or overwhelming to others. You can also become critical of, and impatient with, others who cannot keep up. When combined with high moral standards, your introspection can turn into self-scrutiny.

Intellectual overexcitability is not just about IQ. Since your quest is driven by a need for understanding the unknown and love of truth, rather than external recognitions, your intelligence and rigour are not always reflected in your achievements.

Imaginational overexcitability

With imaginational overexcitability, your mind is imbued with highly original creative and fantastical ideas. You think in terms of images and metaphors; poetry and visual language come naturally to you.

As a child, you had imaginary playmates and pets, and spent long hours in a fantasy world or daydreaming. You have a rich inner world that is the source of your creativity but also your escape. You may appear shy or self-conscious because you spend an extensive amount of time in your inner world.

You are spiritually attuned and may see and perceive things that others don't. You also tend to have idealistic visions that are not shared by others.

Emotional overexcitability

The descriptions of emotional overexcitability overlap with that of a highly sensitive person or hyper-empathic person. You are capable of feeling a wide range of complex emotions to extremes that most people do not reach. This includes both ends of the spectrum – within the course of a day, you may be deep in despair and elated with excitement. You are constantly attuned to the emotional states of others and can be overwhelmed by the amount of information you receive in a group setting or crowded space. With high empathy, you feel like you have to be the emotional caretaker of whatever environment you are in. You form strong emotional ties and attachment to people, places, animals and even objects. Since you feel things more deeply than your friends and partner, a perpetual sense of loneliness lingers.

Psychomotor overexcitability

Psychomotor overexcitability is a heightened excitability of the neuromuscular system. You may talk and move fast, and feel a need for constant motion. Your excessive energy comes out in habits like leg tapping, nail biting or verbal tics. You find yourself acting impulsively or compulsively (such as becoming hyper-organized). You may experience insomnia or a manic state. Since your body fidgets and twitches with excitement in ways that look like hyperactivity, as a child you may have been labelled as having Attention Deficit Hyperactivity Disorder (ADHD).

Sensual overexcitability

Sensual overexcitability is a heightened sensitivity to sound, smell, taste and touch. More than the average person, you derive immense pleasure from visuals, music, colour and other sensory inputs. Simply touching soft surfaces, listening to nature or tasting blasts of flavour in food are hugely pleasing. You appreciate beauty in this world that others miss, such as in art, language and music.

Being stimulated easily also means excessive sensory input overwhelms you. As a child, you did not enjoy many 'normal' social activities due to the high-pitched lighting, insufficient downtime or overwhelming noise. Teachers and parents might have misunderstood you, thinking you were being intentionally difficult.

Since you have a heightened experience of sensual pleasure, you also tend to seek sensual outlets for inner tension. It becomes extra tempting to overindulge in sensual pleasures such as eating, sex and shopping for beautiful things.

The downside of having overexcitabilities is that you are in a constant overdrive. Your brain is always over-intellectualizing and your body is reacting to everything in your environment.[23] When your sympathetic nervous system becomes chronically activated, the constant fight, flight or freeze state can cause immune changes, chronic stress and impact your mood and functioning.

Emotional intensity: gift or mental illness?

Nowadays, we live in an emotion-phobic culture that encourages silencing feelings, especially 'negative' ones. When you are intense, however, the normative strategies of denying, brushing off or dampening down do not work for you. When your friends tell you to 'not think too much', 'go get a drink' or 'just drop it', you do not find their advice helpful. The field of psychology has been dominated by quantitative science and psychiatry, and the definition of mental health has come to be dependent on how well a person can adapt to social norms. Since your 'normal' may appear neurotic and obsessive to others, you may be diagnosed with depression and anxiety.[24] In its extremity, your experience can fall into the criteria for diagnoses such as Borderline/Emotional Dysregulation Personality Disorder, Bipolar Disorder or Attention Deficit Hyperactivity Disorder.

Emotional challenges, from depression to hyperactivity, have always been considered woes by our culture. At the same time, we cannot neglect the fact that many of history's most celebrated innovators and leaders struggled with intense psychological turmoil and mood dysregulation. Mounting research supports the link between traits and behaviours that are considered 'mental disorders' with creativity and high achievement.

A review of clinical studies reveals a recurrent pattern: low to moderate forms of depression, particularly when accompanied by above average IQ, are associated with gifts of empathy, insight and creativity.[25] People with depression get more activation in an area of the brain concerned with altruistic behaviours – called the septal/subgenual cortex.[26] They are more likely than the non-depressed to act in benevolent ways. Other studies have found a link between anxiety and perceptivity, showing that those with an anxiety disorder were more capable of reading facial expressions in others and in picking up their emotions accurately.[27] Apparently, the same dense connections in the brain that cause distress may also be what bring creativity and giftedness.[28] As an emotionally intense person, you have the propensity to plunge into the darker end of our collective consciousness, but it's precisely your ability to feel the pain of the world that gifts you with deep empathy and intuition.

Existential darkness for the highly intense

In a 2012 paper published in *European Psychiatry*, scholar Seubert found that for people who are naturally excitable and intense, conventional methods of understanding depression or therapy are not effective.[29] The depression they have is rarely a pure chemical imbalance, but an existential crisis. It arises from a healthy confrontation with issues such as the meaning of life, justice, isolation, death and their place in the world. Instead of conventional methods, their depression should be understood from the framework of the Theory of Positive Disintegration (TPD) devised by Polish psychiatrist Kazimierz Dąbrowski (1902–1980).

Our society has come to a point where material gains and political power define success; this culture fosters a 'dog-eat-dog' mentality and radical individualism. According to Dąbrowski, contorting oneself to fit into such a 'primitive and confused' world is more unhealthy than feeling uneasy in it.[30] In a world where most people passively accept socialization, the ones who are discontent with the state of affairs became the 'canaries in the coal mine' — the crusaders who feel the woes in the world before everyone else does.

Intense people are perpetually driven by their dissatisfaction with the status quo and the need to push arbitrary limits imposed by traditions or social confines, though this certainly does not mean a glamorous or comfortable life. As a highly sensitive person, because you envision how things could be better, you also painstakingly see how the world, people, institutions and systems fall short of that ideal. You have penetrative insights into the hypocrisies, arbitrariness and dysfunctions in the world, and the gap between reality and your ideals sometimes drives you into loneliness, hopelessness and despair.[31] Before you can transform your anxiety into the materials needed for change, you will likely experience painful inner conflicts. Your depression is not a biological illness, but an indicator of your creative potential. The emotional turmoil you feel is there to help you transition from lower levels of mental functioning to higher levels of personality integration. In *Psychoneurosis is Not an Illness* (1972), Dąbrowski made this point clear: 'Without passing through challenging experiences and even something like psychoneurosis … we cannot realise our multidimensional and multilevel development to higher levels.'[32]

Many great scientists, artists and writers, those who dedicated their life to 'bring light out of darkness' have struggled with existential depression.[33] Abraham Lincoln, Winston Churchill, Carl Jung, Leo Tolstoy, Isaac Newton, Vincent van Gogh, Ludwig Beethoven and Hans Christian Andersen are all examples. At some point in their life, they had a period of physical illness or mental distress, in which they fruitlessly searched for an answer to their emotional problems.[34] It was the 'dark night of the soul' that propelled them to step into their life's purpose.

Lincoln, for instance, responded to his melancholy and break-downs by deciding that he had to fulfil a destiny much greater than he was. Spiritual teacher Eckhart Tolle also experienced a dark period before he reached spiritual awakening, where he simultaneously found a deep sense of peace and deep alive-ness.[35] To him, depression was part of the awakening process, marking the death of the old self and the birth of the true self.

The purpose of presenting the above is not to glorify mental illnesses. Psychiatric input and medications have their place and can be lifesaving. When it comes to the link between mental affliction and creativity, a useful perspective comes from Gail Saltz's work. In her book *The Power of Different*,[36] she pro-poses that there is a 'sweet spot' for expressions of the strengths and abilities associated with brain differences, and this ideal range exists between the extremes of average brain function and acute illness. For example, a person with well-managed mild to moderate bipolar disorder is likely to be more crea-tive than someone with severe bipolar disorder. A person with well-managed ADHD is more likely to thrive in their vocation than someone with an unmanaged condition. Their intensity may be expressed as a mental illness, but is not debilitating enough to take away their ability to turn their pain into art or productivity. This phenomenon goes alongside the empirically supported Yerkes–Dodson law,[37] which states some degree of anxiety enhances performance (but only up to a point).

Our goal, therefore, is to both honour our emotional inten-sity and manage it. It is our best ally if we can see its true nature and make the best of it.

As an intense person, in your life there might not be just one but several cycles of disintegration and renewal. You are an ever-growing, truth-seeking person, so you will always be looking for the next best version of yourself. You test limits and stretch yourself all the time. You are not aware of what you are doing, or that there is a healthy drive behind your inability to compromise. Perhaps a period of chaos and confusion is a rite of passage for the natural non-conformist. Suffering, being alone, self-doubt, sadness and inner conflict are all symptoms of expanding consciousness. Within you is unbounded developmental potential; it is something that you must bring out, or it will rot and swallow you from the inside. Existential depression and bouts of anxiety may be recurring themes of your life, but each time you come through a dark patch, you emerge from the chaos with a new order, new insight, and a new way of being. Each time you come out feeling more deeply alive, and you come closer to your ideal self and to achieving your full potential.

From misfits to leaders

At this stage, you may still be nervous about being labelled as 'gifted', or recoil from the suggestion that you are 'special'. You may fear the extent of your power or be anxious that your new understanding will alienate you from others.

Rather than thinking about your gifts in terms of superiority, it may be more useful to adopt the following perspective: as individuals we all have a unique blueprint. Your way of functioning is rare and not typical, but it is just as nature intended, not any better or worse. As Alan Watts poignantly puts: 'In the spring scenery there is nothing superior, nothing inferior; flowering branches grow naturally, some short, some long. From this standpoint, you see, everybody is seen to be a perfect manifestation of the Godhead or of the void or whatever you want to call it.'[38]

The world we live in today is imbued with crises but also potential. Humanity is calling for a redefinition of power. Increasingly, people yearn to be led by empathy, rather than force. Sensitivity, emotional intensity – what were previously thought of as weaknesses, are now valued qualities that make you stand out. Daniel Pink, in *A Whole New Mind: Why Right-Brainers Will Rule the Future*, he points out that society has arrived at a point in which systematization, computerization and automation are giving way to new skills such as intuition.[39] For more than 100 years, the sequential, linear and logical were praised. As we move towards a different economic era, the world's leaders will need to be innovative thinkers and empathizers.

> As an intense person, you have the potential to be a true game-changer of the world.

Your intellectual curiosity causes you to question, evaluate and scrutinize the existing system. Your sensitivity gives you the ability to feel others' pain and see what help is needed in the world. Your passion for learning equips you with deep knowledge from a wide range of fields. Your imagination allows you to have an ideal vision 'outside the box'. Your energy gives you the stamina and motivation to take action. It is essential to not disown your power and disregard your gifts. When you are born into the world with a fast brain, fierce passion, and the ability to see things clearly and feel things deeply, you are also given the responsibility to harness these as gifts – not just for yourself but also for the greater good.

We live in a time when the emotionally intense misfits are rising to become the leaders. This is by no means an easy task. It requires resilience, courage and the ability to stand up to one's truths. Their first step is a paradigm shift – instead of thinking of yourself as a fragile person who needs to defend themselves against the world, embrace the imperfections in reality and turn your attention to understanding what the world is asking of you. People may still hurt and disappoint you, but you can build your resilience so you can be the bigger person in any situation. It is not through hiding who you are, but by courageously and genuinely meeting with others that you can learn to be tender with sadness, compassionate in darkness, and humble with glory.

Once you have owned your unique life path and qualities, you will realize the gifts you have. By aligning yourself with a bigger purpose, you will also find the strengths that propel you forward. Even if you don't see or feel it right now, the world is waiting for you to shine.

3
Being out-of-sync with the world

Being sensitive and intense points to many gifts – intelligence, intuition, unique talents and creativity. However, being the one who feels when others are numb, the one who voices the truth when others are silent, or the one who thinks deeply about issues others are blind to, makes you an outlier. You may be the misfit, the mystic, the visionary, and that does not lay an easy path in the social world.

There is something in our primitive, tribal nature that causes humans to reject what is different. Although our world as a whole has made huge progress in bridging the divides between class, gender and race, awareness and respect for neuro-divergent traits such as emotional intensity have not broken through into public consciousness.

> As a society we continue to pathologize individuals who are different.

Being in the presence of an outlier challenges people to question their existing belief system, and not many are ready for that. People who have a high level of openness are more likely to embrace diversity.[1] Those who are themselves sensitive, imaginative and in touch with their feelings usually align with the idea that we do not have to all think, feel and act in uniformity, and may come to appreciate the unique angle and energy the highly sensitive person brings to the group. However, we cannot always control who we are surrounded by. Some of us are born into authoritarian and close-minded families; we may be put into schools with rigid standards, or be stuck in a workplace with an insensitive or toxic culture.

Unfortunately, when people look for a scapegoat, the one who is the most sensitive and 'quirky' by nature is often assigned the role. The intellectually intense child who eagerly blurts out answers in the classroom is considered disruptive; their inability to sustain attention on mundane subjects is deemed as defiant. As an adult, rigorous intellectual pursuits or a preference for solitude may be misinterpreted as being aloof, arrogant, a social recluse, or even clinically 'schizoid'.

Modern psychiatry also handles intensity in a narrow fashion. To apply labels and diagnoses to people, clinicians and therapists have relied on standardized manuals and rigid protocols. Your high energy might be interpreted as Attention Deficit Hyperactivity Disorder, your intense emotions diagnosed as Borderline Personality Disorder, your bouts of creative obsession as Bipolar Disorder, your perfectionism as Obsessive-Compulsive Disorder and your existential depression is mistaken as clinical depression. Of course, people who are born intense and sensitive are not immune from medical disorders. However, the natural characteristics of intense people can look like pathology even when there is not any.

You might have tried, again and again, to fit in, without much success. Perhaps in school, you tried to be a part of the popular clique, but could not tolerate the small talk or the lack of depth in pseudo-friendships. True peers are hard to come by, and perhaps you struggle to find people with whom you can share freely and spontaneously, without being accused of being 'too much', 'too fast' or 'too complex'. At work, people might be threatened by your honesty; you either have to silence yourself or 'manage your manager'. You might be the 'black sheep' of the family, and your chosen life path is not respected by them. After years of being misdiagnosed by health professionals, and misunderstood by even those who are close to you, it may have become difficult for you to reclaim your natural gifts.

The following paragraphs summarize some of the core struggles of being an exceptionally intense and sensitive person in the world. Before you move forward, however, it is paramount that you understand the following: although it hurts to be alienated, it is not because you have done anything wrong, or that there is anything fundamentally wrong with you. However much you want to fit in, it is not worth sacrificing your values and integrity. You might have internalized shame, but it is misplaced. One of the goals of this journey is to reclaim your dignity, so you are no longer held back by your parents', siblings' or society's judgement and projections.

Your struggles in the world

Differences in temperament is a determining factor of the quality of family life. The 'goodness of fit' between the parents' and the child's natural temperaments decides how hard they have to work to get along.[2] Challenges arise when an intense child is born into a family in which the parents or siblings do not function in the same way. Imagine being an active, exuberant and emotional child in a family with parents and siblings who are slow to respond or conflict-avoidant, or being a sensitive child in an extraverted, 'thick-skinned' household.

Being the apple that fell far from the tree

In *Far From the Tree: Parents, Children and the Search for Identity*, researcher Andrew Solomon discusses the differences between directly inherited (vertical) and independently divergent (horizontal) identity.[3] Most children share at least some traits with their family: tall parents are likely to have tall children; people who speak Greek raise their children to speak Greek. These attributes and values are passed down from parent to child across the generations through DNA and cultural norms, and are known as 'vertical identities'. In contrast, when we have a trait that is foreign to our parents, it is referred to as 'a horizontal identity'. Horizontal identities may include being gay, having a physical disability, having autism, being exceptionally sensitive, intense, or being intellectually or empathically gifted. Unfortunately, vertical identities are normally respected while horizontal identities are treated as flaws. Unconventional ways of being are often disparaged as 'illnesses' to be fixed.

It is difficult for parents to have children with ways of being and needs that are alien to them. 'Parenthood abruptly catapults us into a permanent relationship with a stranger' wrote Solomon in describing the dynamic in these families.[4] All children need emotionally attuned caregivers who can be emotionally available and responsive. This is an essential building block for the child's development, and determines their future emotional intelligence and self-regulation ability.[5] When children are born intense and sensitive, they have even higher emotional needs. Since they have a 'sharp radar' that intuitively picks up what is going on in their surroundings, they can sense parents' disregard from their microexpressions or non-verbal cues. Given their sensory sensitivities, they need extra support in self-regulation to not be constantly overwhelmed by environmental stimuli. For these children, having parents who know how to support them provides a necessary 'safe harbour'; even when their peers reject them, or their teachers misunderstand them, they have a place to go back to for solace and comfort. Families of emotionally intense children are presented with a fork in the road: they can reject or scapegoat their child or they can rise to the occasion and allow themselves to be changed by their experience. Unfortunately, under the influence of a culture that is inept at embracing diversity, some parents have come to perceive their child's emotional intensity as not just a problem but a personal failure or even insult. Even with the best intentions, not all parents can do the latter. Having emotionally unavailable, cold or critical parents is detrimental to the psyche of all children, but the impact is worse on innately sensitive children.

The 'apple fallen far from the tree' phenomenon applies not just to the parents but also the rest of the family. Research has found that siblings likely share similarities in physical characteristics and cognitive abilities; when it comes to personality, however, we are similar to our siblings only about 20 per cent of the time. This might be a surprising finding to some, but the odds for us to be similar to our siblings in terms of personality is almost identical to that with strangers.[6] This means that if you are born intense and sensitive, there is only a small chance that your siblings will share the same characteristics. In situations where you are the only emotionally sensitive person in the household, you easily become the minority and a likely target of scapegoating.

Your family is the first 'group' you experience in life, and your experience shapes your future perception of yourself in a group. Attachment theories state that your early experience forms your 'internal working model', which colours all your future attachment-related behaviours, thoughts and feelings.[7] If, growing up, you were largely marginalized, neglected or scapegoated, or if you have been told you are too demanding all your life, as an adult it is difficult to shake off the unconscious expectation that what you have been told or have experienced so far will be your future.

The coping strategies a person adopts to survive in a family home where they do not fit in shapes their personality. For instance, you may have used humour to cope, and you now adopt the 'class clown' role wherever you go. If you have learned from your childhood experience that being vulnerable is not safe, you may not be able to put your guard down even when you want to. Perhaps as a child you sought love by being helpful and compliant, and are now stuck in the same pattern struggling with boundaries and co-dependent relationships. These patterns may serve as a coping mechanism for a while, but eventually they will keep you from living a full life.

Becoming the target of envy

While many books have been written about sensitive people, one subject that is little discussed is the potential and implications of being the target of envy.

The psychodynamic of envy is subtle, and the person experiencing envy may not realize what is driving them. In fact, studies have found that most people are not consciously aware of their own envy – furthermore the stronger it is, the more likely they are to suppress it.[8] Since people typically only envy people who share a similar background, we are most likely to become the target of envy from our peers and siblings. Research has also found we are more likely to be envious of those of the same sex.[9]

It may come as a surprise that others might be envious of you, but as we saw in the last chapter, being an intense person and giftedness are related. Many intense people possess unique qualities or talents that others wish they had. For example, people who are not able to be forthright with their innermost feelings can resent you for your ability to tell the truth. Others may be envious of your intuition, creativity or artistic capabilities.

Envy happens whether or not it is rational or justified. Your siblings may envy you for your beauty or intelligence, even if you did not choose to possess these qualities. Your parents may make the situation worse by undermining you in order to equalize the power dynamic. Family members may reflect that you possess 'a certain kind of quality' that is hard to pin down but is best described as a penetrative spiritual acumen. They may have sensed this in you since you were little. Feeling intimidated by your powerful presence, adults in your life may find ways to shut you down. They might ask you to be quiet, or suggest you keep your head down or keep your thoughts and positive feelings to yourself. Harry Potter is an archetypal example of what it means to be a gifted child and the target of toxic envy in his family.

Research has found that when people envy someone, they will socially undermine their target.[10] This creates a situation where, either covertly or overtly, a family or a work team gangs up against one member. Seemingly rational justifications or reasons might be created to support the oppression, and this can be done in ways that are disguised as 'for your own good'. They may say, 'We need to toughen you up for your own sake', 'Being sensitive is not good for you' or even 'We are helping you to correct your faulty personality'.

As a highly sensitive and intense person, it is understandable that you have adapted yourself to deal with the threat of envy. Theories and research show that we go to great lengths to down-regulate other people's envy if we want to preserve the relationship and feel threatened by potential hostility from the envier.[11] Both conditions are likely met in the cases of our family and peers. In a perennial anthropological analysis of envy, Foster (1972) describes a few approaches we commonly adopt to moderate envy.[12] They include:

- Concealment: hiding who we are or any signs of advantage
- Denial: downplaying our joy
- Compensating: in some way to the envious person.

Another common reaction to being envied is appeasement, where we become people pleasers and avoid conflicts at all cost.[13]

If you have been told since a young age that your thoughts and feelings are not valid, you have probably learned to silence yourself. If whenever you stand out you are undermined or criticized, you will eventually internalize this oppression. This can manifest in adulthood as self-sabotaging behaviours (for example, turning down a promotion, not going for an opportunity that requires you to speak up), extreme self-consciousness or social anxiety. Your original personality becomes hidden under layers of anxiety. Even if you now want to fulfil your full potential, and step out of these self-limiting cycles of self-sabotage, you may no longer know how.

Being the unwelcome messenger

Intense people tend to be perfectionists who set high standards for themselves and others, and this extends to moral standards. If you are such a person, you will have a high degree of honesty and integrity and will often be the first to notice ethical breaches and speak up for injustice. You are the whistleblower when faced with an inconvenient truth while others stay complacent. You are the one who stands up to authorities in an unfair work situation or the one to 'tell it as it is' in your family. You question traditions and challenge authorities, not because you want to cause trouble but because arbitrary rules do not make sense to you. Deep down, you have a sincere desire to enlighten others with what needs to be known and to improve the state of the world.

As an intuitive person, you also spot patterns that are not obvious to the naked eye. You have penetrating insights about other people's psychology and are aware of things they are not aware of themselves. When you were younger, you said things that shocked the adults around you – because they were uncomfortably real. Unfortunately, just because something is right does not mean it is welcome, and most people are not ready for the truth. Social science research has shown that 'shooting the messenger' is a real phenomenon.

Because of its social advantages, most people choose to deny reality and avoid a psychologically uncomfortable truth.[14]

When a moral truth-teller disrupts the existing equilibrium, they are considered a threat.[15] When they point out something that contradicts people's existing beliefs, attitudes or opinions, it creates cognitive dissonance and their input is unwelcome.[16] For many visionaries across time and space, it may take a long time before their contribution is accepted. In more unfortunate cases, they are cast out from the group before that time comes. If this has happened repeatedly in your life, you may start to assume there is something wrong with you, and you may also start to devalue your worth.

If this has been your experience, it may have become difficult for you to trust yourself, but your unique perspective is exactly what the world needs. What you offer is the catalyst for positive change. Even if those in your immediate surroundings do not honour you right now, you must hold on to your values and beliefs, and proactively find a channel for your voice.

> There are people in the world waiting to be connected with you, to know that there is someone like them, and to be saved by what you have to say.

If you dim your light for the mockers, you deprive those who are ready to receive your message. Even if you don't yet believe in yourself, believe in those who believe in you. It may be the hardest thing you ever have to do, but you must honour your truth even when no one else does. Ultimately, the pain of leaving this world without having been who you ought to be is much greater than losing approval from the herd.

Not finding true peers

Your intensity might mean it is more difficult for you to connect in a true way with your peers. Your intellectual rigour, combined with your spiritual awareness, translate into depth and complexity that few can match. Your mind runs on multiple tracks and you think faster than you speak. You can be impatient with others when they fail to grasp information as quickly as you do, or are not aware of things you think of as common sense. Boredom is a perennial struggle for intense people. Even if you are an extrovert, parties or networking events may bore you, as the conversations in these settings remain shallow and do not feed your soul. You might have an unorthodox sense of humour and come across as socially awkward. Perhaps you are hurt or feel let down when others don't 'get it'. Even with their best intentions, your parents can leave you feeling spiritually alone, or you don't feel stimulated by your romantic partner. Your frustration comes out as irritation, and others may see you as aloof or arrogant.

You may start blaming yourself for your dissatisfaction. You ask yourself, 'Am I too demanding, unreasonable, arrogant?', 'Why am I not able to lower my expectations?', 'What is wrong with me that I cannot find another person like me?' To survive the dissatisfactory social world, you may have intentionally dulled your senses. You hide your qualities and no longer seek places where your quirks and creativity will be celebrated; instead, you put a mask on and pretend to be like everyone else. However, you soon find that the sense of isolation or despair grows rather than diminishes.

Another consequence of being a fast-moving creature is that you continuously find yourself outgrowing the people around you. With an immense drive to better yourself, growth comes to you at lightning speed. As you expand psychologically and spiritually, you find that you no longer have anything in common with your childhood peers, your family of origin or intimate partners. You are continuously invited to release what no longer has the same place in your life; it may be a person, an idea, a habit or a community. Change, however, is never easy. You may think departing means betraying, or that letting go means you are selfish. However, just because letting go feels painful does not mean you are doing anything wrong. With self-compassion, see if you can hold the grief gently in your heart, without letting it stop you from taking the next step. Through the journey in this book, I hope you can reach a point where you are free from guilt, shame or the compulsion to rescue anyone. Trust that you are going in the right direction and that as long as your intention is sincere and you act with integrity, the process will take care of itself.

Not walking a conventional path

Many intense people have an unconventional life or career trajectory. Unconventional means not making life choices based on traditions or what everyone else does, but on authentic needs and desires. Breaking free of conformity means living by your truth, even when it is uncomfortable.

You might be a 'multipotentialite'[17] or a polymath who has many interests but not 'one true calling'. With a wide range of interests, a strong drive to learn and a love for intellectual stimulation, you haven't lost your childlike sense of wonder when it comes to a new pursuit. Human society used to celebrate polymaths: Leonardo Da Vinci, Issac Newton, Galileo, Aristotle and Charles Darwin are all famous generalists. However, since the Industrial Revolution, specializing has become what conventional wisdom prescribes. Those who are unable to settle on one path for life are now criticized as 'not trying hard enough', being 'spoilt', 'feeling entitled' or 'immature'.

You may be a spiritual seeker in a consumerist world, a late bloomer in your academic and career path, a single parent, an entrepreneur, a self-starter, an artist, a hermit, a nomad, a lifelong traveller. You might have adopted a non-conventional relationship or family configuration, or chosen to stay single. In other words, you have taken the path less travelled, whether or not it was a conscious choice – what you do, how you live, where you live and what you believe in falls outside of the mainstream.

When you swim against the flow, you are faced with resistance; this can be in the form of silent judgements, back-handed criticism, or even well-meaning advice and pressure. As Chris Guillebeau states in his book *The Art of Non-Conformity*, adjectives such as 'unreasonable', 'unrealistic' and 'impractical' are all words used to marginalize a person or idea that fails to conform with conventionally expected standards.[18]

Taking the conventional path offers easy access to a ready-made community, while being the wild card requires hard work in seeking connections and kinship. If it gets too difficult, you may be pushed to drop what is authentic to you and opt for the normative path. Your genuine desires, however, are not simply extinguished. At some point, you will hear the call from the depth of your psyche, calling you to return to your truth.

The wounds of not belonging

Social psychologists have long agreed that the need to belong is a fundamental motivation and is present in all humans in all cultures.[19] It does not come as a surprise, therefore, that being rejected is related to a wide range of psychological outcomes.[20] It can affect your ability to perform,[21] how lonely you feel,[22] levels of self-esteem[23] and your propensity to depression.[24]

As an intense person, your complex mind and drive amplify social anxiety and hypervigilance. When you are anxious, your attention to detail, perfectionism and critical thinking skills converge to work against you. You may overthink and dissect the fine points of all your interactions, and allow your self-defeating behaviours to run rampant. You may also become a 'chameleon' in social groups, even if it means losing touch with your authentic self. Research has found that being rejected activates the 'monitoring system' in your psyche, causing you to become extra sensitized to social information such as other people's emotional vocal tone and facial expressions.[25] Furthermore, when you are socially excluded, your tendency towards 'non-conscious behavioural mimicry' increases; this is when you mimic the behaviours of others without awareness or conscious control.[26] Perhaps unconsciously, you think that by talking and acting like the in-group members, you will be accepted. Before you know it, you have lost touch with the ability to speak and act spontaneously and of your own accord.

When the pain of being ostracized gets too much, many of us resort to numbing ourselves out in order to cope. This mechanism is reflected in not just our psychology but also physiology. Recent findings indicate social exclusion activates the same area of the brain that responds to physical pain.[27] Surprisingly, study after study has found that being socially excluded leads to a decrease, rather than an increase, in physical pain sensitivity. The same pattern is found in the animal kingdom: studies in animal literature have shown that a variety of animals respond to social isolation with decreased sensitivity to pain.[28] This numbness can extend to an emotional level,[29] which may have helped you to survive the pain of not belonging at the beginning but, in the long run, it leads to a state of chronic dissociation, where you feel nothing but lethargic, empty and devoid of any aliveness.[30]

It is okay to not fit in

Embracing your non-conformity is potentially the most profound and powerful mental shift you can make.

All your life, you have tried to 'fit in', but what if what your deepest self needs is authenticity, rather than false belongingness? You might have spent your whole life thinking there is something wrong with you for being different, but what if you are an inspiration? We no longer live in homogenous tribes and villages, and exposure to diversity is inevitable. By honouring your idiosyncrasies and demonstrating self-acceptance, you are allowing others to do the same.

Perhaps your seat in this world, however much you fight it, is indeed on the fringe. You can find tremendous peace and relief in coming to terms with the fact that you will never quite 'fit in' in a conventional setting when it comes to social norms and what the majority does. It is undoubtedly challenging to be a non-conformist, but just because the majority and authorities reject you, does not mean there is something wrong with you. You are different, yes. But that doesn't make you bad, wrong, defective in any way. You will be misunderstood and sidelined, but that still does not make your values and the way you are inferior in any way.

Honing the skill to survive other people's judgements is an ongoing practice. It involves you learning to stay grounded in self-love, your core values and beliefs, and to have an inner circle of those who see and accept you. Sometimes, though not always, the price of being authentic is to accept that you cannot please everyone. You may attract toxic envy, negative projections and criticisms. However, if your number one goal in life is to play it safe, you may just stifle your own potential. Before you shrink your soul and are at the mercy of others' acceptance, be clear about what is truly important to you.

Life is finite and, at the end of your time, only a handful of people will matter. Do you have to exert energy pleasing everyone on your path?

Perhaps you have never felt at home wherever you go. But your true home is not your biological family, the small town you were born in, nor the big city you live in. Your true home is not a particular person nor group nor place, but the 'moments of meetings' when you intellectually, emotionally and spiritually connect. It lies beyond the physical, the biological or what you can see. It is when your soul aligns with a piece of writing, art or music, and when you are inspired, transformed, elevated. It is when you download materials from a source bigger than yourself, and when you express yourself freely and unapologetically.

Becoming okay with not being 'normal' initially brings grief but, alongside your sadness, there is an undercurrent of relief – finally you can stop trying to be what you are not, and gone is the burden of false impressions. With a new slate, what might life bring when you are just you? What people, possibilities may you attract now? It is only by reclaiming your true self can you embark on a path to find true belongingness – where you will be accepted without having to pretend, and shine without fearing retaliation. It is time to allow your emotions and interest to run free range, let yourself fully appreciate your abilities, accept your unique interests and allow yourself to truly be at home. You will never be homeless, exiled or betrayed if you can find your true home from within.

In the following chapters, more specific advice will be given regarding various settings and spheres of your life. Chapter 5 will discuss how you can negate the challenges in your family life, Chapter 6 will deal with your challenges in romantic relationships, and in Chapter 7 we will see some specific things you can do when people at work don't get you and how to negate the pain and consequences of not fitting in.

PART 2

From hiding to thriving

4

The relationship with yourself

Reclaiming authenticity is a rite of passage for the natural misfits. Intensity and sensitivity are tremendous gifts, but without the right understanding and support, having an operating system that is out-of-sync can result in many shameful experiences. If your parents, teachers or peers were impatient or critical towards your quirks, you might have assumed you were in the wrong. You believed that not fitting in meant there was something wrong with you – that it was you who needed to change. If this is the case, eventually, you disown your intensity and lose touch with your essence. At some point in your life, however, you will be called back to your true nature. The call may be as a result of a significant transition: moving to a new country, a critical illness, the end of a career, the departure of something or someone dear to you. Then, you realize that it is not enough to exist as just a projection of your spouse, parents, friends or society, and that you must reclaim your intuitive and empathic soul. In this chapter, we will walk you through the sacred process of your transformation, from forcing yourself to fit in where you do not to finding true belongingness.

Becoming your true self

When you were small, safety meant doing all you could to avoid abandonment. Since you were dependent on your parents for survival, you had to please them and avoid any risk of rejection, even if it meant silencing your needs. When you were a teenager, belonging meant adapting to the world. You did everything you could to avoid bullying or teasing. As an adult, you are the chameleon that changes colour to fit in. You make yourself useful, efficient and productive, so you won't be ignored. You have become hypervigilant, picking up on the smallest negative social clues and editing yourself accordingly. In the past, your vibrancy and excitement were met with blind stares and puzzlement; through experience you realized sharing yourself made you feel more lonely than not. The minute your achievements stand out, they get chopped down; so, you learned to never reach high. Opportunities become threats, and you may just self-sabotage before anyone has a chance to destroy you.

You thought you could protect yourself by acting small, but stifling your soul comes with huge costs. You may end up with a career that offers material security but requires you to disown your creativity, or you become trapped in a practical but soulless relationship. You have constant inner conflicts and feel confused about your identity and desires. You are not able to feel joy and pleasure, and wake up in the morning feeling unmotivated and nihilistic. You are like a wild animal trying to domesticate itself, trading your natural exuberance for the crowd's approval. Deep down, however, you know you are not living up to your full potential, and feel guilty of letting life slip past without fully experiencing it.

True self, false self

The idea of a 'True Self' versus a 'False Self' was first introduced by British psychoanalyst D.W. Winnicott in 1960 to explain how we forgo our authenticity for survival.[1] Your True Self is your most innocent, spontaneous and creative self; it is who you were as a child when you felt safe in the presence of a trusted other and were free to express yourself. In contrast, the False Self is a defensive facade, something you created to meet the demands of your parents, other people and society.

Your facade started as a means to meet your needs, but it has overstayed its welcome and become the only thing you know. The consequence of over-investing in your False Self is that you become physically and psychologically sick. When your outside self is succumbing to conformity, your inner being becomes silently deviant. If you do not address the issue, this underlying rebellion will push back and erupt. That is why you sometimes 'act out' with explosive and destructive behaviour, without knowing why.

Like Winnicott's notion of the 'False Self', Carl Jung used the term 'Persona' to describe the ego identity we build in the first half of our lives.[2] *Persona* is Latin for 'mask'; it is your interface with the outer world, a compromise between your honest self and society's many 'shoulds'. While it is not a problem to have some distinctions between your private life and your socialized self, you run the risk of becoming completely fused with your mask. Just like a fish can't see the water because it's in it, so you may not discern the unconscious values, doctrines and cultural rules that govern your life. You do not see how much you have invested in a path that is not truly yours: the corporate job, the glamorous relationship, a well-endorsed 'extraverted' personality. To keep up your facade, you suppress anger and deny joy, and in the end, even your spontaneity and creative energy go into hiding.

> The good news is that your soul might have been shielded,
> but it has not disappeared.

Your intensities do not cease to exist just because your family, school, church and social conventions disregard them. You may have overworked your suit of armour, but eventually your truths will wake you up, sometimes at surprising times. Jung found that people often suffer from anxiety or depression at the midpoint of their lives (which for the old souls can mean anything from mid-twenties to late-fifties) because they are 'sick of normalization'.[3] When you can no longer hide from your truth, it is actually a sign of health.

The death of your old self

Reclaiming your identity as a sensitive and intense person is the first step in your transformation from hiding to thriving. In all transformations, you release something old to make room for something new. Your false self must 'die' before your true self can be reborn. Alongside some relationships, titles and career paths, you also need to forgo long-held beliefs, ideas about what the future holds, and who you thought you were.

With the letting go of your old identity, you enter a chaotic 'liminal space' – a space where you float in an 'in-between' zone. Mystics call this period the 'dark night of the soul' (Saint John of the Cross, 2007).[4] In this disconcerting time, what you have learned through your family, education and the social order no longer holds up to your questioning. More and more, what seemed 'normal' looks hypocritical, insufficient or unethical. Your previous drivers – survival fears, the need to prove yourself, the reliance on external approval – drop away. Others may not understand the change in you. Since you live in a culture that values forward movement and productivity, being detached from these ego-driven ideals leaves you in an isolated position. If you then try to resolve this challenge through conventional wisdom and taking traditional advice from others, you will find that these old ways have ceased to help.

With the death of your old self, you may cycle back and forth between the 'stages of grieving' that were suggested by Kübler-Ross (1973): Denial, Anger, Bargaining, Depression, Acceptance:[5]

- Denial: I am sure I am not that different. I can do what everyone else does. As my parents said, maybe I didn't try hard enough (to fit in).

- Anger: Why me? Why does it seem easy for others and not me? Why do I try so hard but still not get where I want to be? Life is not fair! Why can't the world be a bit more understanding?
- Bargaining: Let me give it another go to fit in. I will try this way, and that way.
- Depression: This is hopeless. I am a misfit. I will never feel happy and fulfilled. Why do I bother?
- Acceptance: I am who I am. Even though it is sometimes not easy to be more intense and sensitive than others, I trust that my authenticity will allow the right people, position, and situation to come to me.

Two kinds of fear

As you are about to break through, two types of fear may drive you away from your authentic path: the fear of the past and the fear of the future.

Fear of the past means you are fearful about 'coming out' as who you are because you don't want history to repeat itself. This is how conventional psychotherapy understands the nature of anxiety. Maybe your exuberance was once neglected or punished by your parents. Perhaps outshining your peers has caused you to be bullied and oppressed. You were once humiliated without the words to fight back, and the trauma was stored in your body. Now, as you launch yourself into authenticity, the historical terror of ostracization and powerlessness surges back like a tornado.

On the other hand, from an existentialist perspective, you are haunted by the potential of a wide-open future. It is overwhelming to imagine what new opportunities might arise if you allow yourself to live as you are, and allow your interests and intense emotions to roam free. In the philosopher Sartre's (1957) words, you fear the 'vertigo of possibility' – you almost cannot stand the excitement.[6] It may sound paradoxical at first that you would worry about your freedom, but with freedom comes responsibilities. To acknowledge that you do have a choice also means you are accountable for your actions. You have to be grown-up about your choices, commit to the life you have chosen and grieve what you have let go. This is a daunting task.

Society's pressure does not make your renewal process any easier. Often when you take a step towards authenticity, people in your family and community will dismiss, underestimate or criticize you. They feel threatened by the truth, as it exposes what they are not facing in their own lives. Your emergence is a threat to the stability of the existing system, and either consciously or unconsciously people will attempt to bring things back to the status quo.

Confronted by the fear of the past and the future, you try to hold on to a false sense of certainty. You may run away from the void by resorting to your old defence mechanisms.

> If, when presented with the doorway to liberation, you do
> not trust it, what you end up rejecting is not only change,
> but also life itself.

Your invitation

Mental chaos is also a rite of passage as you step into your full potential. Many great artists and thinkers have to go through this to find their voices and to put their unique stamp on the world. Carl Jung developed his theory of individualization out of his own painful personal experience. Being the son of a pastor in the Swiss Reformed Church, he discovered early in his life that he could not subscribe to the Orthodox Protestant faith in which he had been raised. He had to forge his own path. He did this again in later life when he disagreed with his long-term friend and mentor, Sigmund Freud. Given Freud's prominence in the 1920s, Jung's action required tremendous strength.

In Joseph Campbell's seminal book *Hero with a Thousand Faces*, he suggests that the great myths of the world all have very similar plot lines; he summarizes them into what he called the 'hero's journey'.[7] All heroes, in their pursuit of deep meaning, first leave the familiar world; then there is a pivotal moment in their story where they stand alone. They may be ostracized or rejected at first, but ultimately it is their willingness to rebel and push back that cures the world of its collective sickness, numbness and blindness. As Hermann Hesse puts it: 'My story isn't pleasant, it's not sweet and harmonious like the invented stories; it tastes of folly and bewilderment, of madness and dream, like the life of all people who no longer want to lie to themselves.'[8]

Chaos is a part of your growth. When you feel anxious or depressed, do not jump to a belief that you are sick. You might just be on the brink of awakening.

In the dark wood, courage means something different to everyone. Something simple for others may require great strength from you. You may not like or feel comfortable with what is happening, but you can work on staying open to the process and letting it unfold. Success belongs to those who have the ability to ride the inevitable waves of discomfort that come with change, and still stay put. However tempting it is to run away, you must not numb but befriend your many emotions – including grief, disappointment and anger. They are not your enemies but messengers from your psyche. When you remain still but open, life speaks to you.

You must also find patience and self-compassion, and not blame yourself for things that are happening or have happened in the past. A part of you may wish you had taken action sooner but, like everything in nature, your life path must work in cycles and seasons. All that you have done up to now is a valuable exploration that sets the foundation for your success. You could not have known until you knew, you could not have leapt until you were ready. You have been doing exactly 'the right thing' all along.

Think of your transformation as a shift in your centre of gravity – from doing to being, from the material to the spiritual. You are moving from an unexamined life to your inner castle. As you wake up to the falsity of the world, you become an original thinker with your own approach to resolving paradoxes in the world. The result of your productive conflict is a renewed sense of independence and integrity. Being grounded in your truth also frees you up to manifest your gifts and talents through words, art, meaningful domestic endeavours or social actions. There is nothing narcissistic about living authentically – quite the opposite. It takes humility to be real. It is a noble act when you focus not on feeding your own need to be liked, but on setting an example for other sensitive and intense souls. Your brave move allows others to do the same, making your coming out a meaningful, transpersonal process.

Instead of finding guidance from those geographically close to you, you may have to find soulmates by reading books and biographies and learning from kindred spirits across time and space. You can also connect with spirituality through writing, journaling, or creating art or music. Ultimately, you will learn to rely on yourself to console, reassure, comfort and nurture your own soul. Even when there is no one exactly like you in your immediate surroundings, you can be your own ally.

I want to end this chapter with an invitation – for you to see your emotional crisis in a different light, and to learn to honour your existential darkness. Despite it being a precarious journey, it is worthwhile. Your doubtful moment is a critical juncture of your growth – either you give yourself a chance to reclaim your identity as a sensitive and intense person, or you continue to live a lie. If you can hold on and stay on your path, you will descend into the depth of your psyche to reconnect with your deepest essence. True belonging does not come from disowning any parts of you. By integrating all aspects within, including the anger, sadness, creativity and vitality you have previously rejected, you become a whole human. At the end of chaos, you will find a new level of intimacy with life, yourself and other people.

Reflective exercise: your eulogies

'Memento mori' is a Latin phrase that literally means 'remember death'. As a practice, it means to contemplate our own mortality, and the brevity and fragility of human life. It may seem paradoxical at first glance, but for sages, philosophers and artists from across time and space, the death meditation is a tried-and-true antidote to much of our human suffering, including death anxiety itself.

Remembering that our time is finite helps us to stay in the present moment, re-focus on our deepest values, and motivates us to relinquish fixations on things that are ultimately trivial and transient in nature. The ancient Stoic philosophers used the meditation on death to stimulate courage, humility, moderation and other virtues. In this exercise, you are encouraged to contemplate your own mortality, in order to focus on and harness the best of what you do have – the gift of life.

Make sure that you set aside at least an hour for this exercise. Find a quiet place, where you will not be interrupted. Start by closing your eyes, and take a few deep breaths.

Imagine that you have come to the end of your life. For some miraculous reason, you are able to witness your own funeral from above. Visualize what it looks like. Where will it be? Will it be indoor or outdoor? Who will be there? See their faces, and the expressions on their faces. You can have many or a few people at your funeral, there is no limit.

Now, imagine that someone close to you stands up to tell others what they remember about you. They will speak about who you were, what you stood for, how you have lived, what made your path unique, how you made people around you feel, and what you have brought to the world.

For the first part of this exercise, write your eulogy as if your life ended today. Think about people you have met in the past and what they may say about you. Take a moment to celebrate all that you have done so far, but also think about the unfulfilled hopes and dreams if you leave the world at this very moment. Be as honest as possible, even if some of the truths hurt.

Now, imagine some years had passed, and you have died as an older person. This time, write your eulogy as you would ideally like it. Think about your legacy, the meaning you have created in the world, lives you have touched, and all of your contributions. What does it mean to have a well-lived life? What would you want to be remembered for? Can you summarize your messages in a few sentences?

As much as possible, think beyond external achievements, and focus on the qualities and values you want to have manifested.

Now, read back on what you have written.

- Did anything surprise you?
- What does this process reveal about your inner and outer world?
- What do you know about your values and strengths?
- How may the outcome of this exercise inform your life today?
- When you put things in perspective, what current worries, preoccupations or hang-ups would you choose to drop?

Finally, set aside the eulogies you have written. In your journal, reflect on and answer the following questions:

- What am I like at my most innocent, trusting, playful and spontaneous?
- How has being naive hurt me in the past?
- At what point did I start putting a wall up?
- What does safety mean to me?
- What does power mean to me?
- How has tradition and cultural baggage affected my life?
- What internal rules might be unconsciously governing my life?
- What social confines have I broken through and what backlash has come as a result of that?
- At the moment, is my soul knocking on my conscience? Is there a trumpet sounding from within that I am pretending not to hear?
- What gifts do I have that are uniquely mine?
- What is the worst that can happen if I were to tell the world about these gifts?
- If I am completely honest with myself, what relationships will I have to let go of?
- If I am completely honest with myself, what opportunities may I open my door to?
- At this juncture of my life, what do I have to grieve? What do I have to celebrate?
- What are my core values? What in me remains unchanged regardless of external circumstances?
- What ideas or fixed mindsets have expired and can be let go of?
- What new beliefs or values can I now live by?
- If I only have ten/five/one more year(s) to live, what will I change?

Should you control your emotions?

Being emotionally intense does not mean being unstable, but if you have not yet learned to regulate your emotions, you may feel overwhelmed by the constant stream of complex emotions you feel every day. Bouts of obsessive thoughts, panic attacks, spirals of shame or intense fear of abandonment may visit you at random hours, taking you by surprise. On some days, you may wake up in the morning to one of these unwelcome guests without knowing why.

For a long time, you have thought your task is to 'control' or get on top of your emotions. You might have looked everywhere for strategies to dilute your anger, activities that will dampen your anxiety, or stimulants that will lessen your depression. However, the results are that you either become numb and dissociated, or start to constantly fight your own mind. When swinging between the two extremes, you will have little peace in-between.

In this chapter, we will look at what you can do when you have a complex and turbulent emotional landscape. What you will realize is that, although you have little control over the thoughts, feelings and sensations that emerge from inside you, you do have a choice in how you relate to and deal with them. Through developing a healthy relationship with your feelings, you can ride the waves of intensity with both passion and peace, without resorting to numbness or chaos.

'Feel good only'?

Our modern world fosters a 'feel good only' culture. From a young age, our parents asked us to 'be quiet and stop crying', and we are made to feel ashamed of showing anger or sadness in public. When we look around, magazines and self-help books are full of advice on how to 'control anger', or 'get rid of sadness'.

Everywhere we go, we receive the message that some emotions are flaws to get rid of, or inconveniences to grow out of.

Within the healthcare system, achieving mental health involves labelling someone with a 'disorder' and prescribing them with pills to dampen feelings. Some therapists encourage their patients to categorize emotions as either rational or irrational, and then try to exert control over them. What makes it worse is when we are told to banish certain feelings but are not able to do so, and end up in a loop of self-blame and distress. As a result, we become at war with ourselves.

Emerging research has found that the 'feel good' approach makes the problem worse. Increasingly, psychologists and therapists have realized that suffering comes not from the experience of emotional pain, but from our attempts to avoid it. It turns out that instead of trying to make unpleasant feelings go away, by learning to live with them, ideally with an attitude of friendliness, we can attain psychological and physical well-being.[9] This understanding has given rise to what is known as the 'third wave' of cognitive behavioural therapies, such as Acceptance and Commitment Therapy, Dialectical Behaviour Therapy, Compassion-focused Therapy and Mindfulness-Based Cognitive Therapy. In these models, the elements of mindfulness, acceptance and compassion are introduced. The therapeutic goal is not to run away from unpleasant thoughts and feelings, but to live with them in a non-judgemental, positive way.

If what you have been doing so far is not working, it is time to try a different approach. For someone with a rich but turbulent emotional world, the conventional advice of 'ignore and suppress' is rarely sufficient. As you may have realized by now, when it comes to your feelings you cannot swim against the tide, no matter how hard you try. Learning to accept and befriend your stream of emotions is much more sustainable than being in a constant tug-of-war with them.

How to be with your emotions

When you are faced with challenging emotions, your gut reaction is either to run away from them (through suppression, repression, detachment or spiritual by-passing), or to over-analyse and be at war with them. Neither of these ways will work in the long run, because genuine wellbeing is found when you can hold the paradox of engagement and detachment without resorting to extremes. In this new approach, your task is not to get rid of your emotions, but to make space for them and allow the natural physio-psychological process to take place with little interruption. Then, you may find that your emotions will calm down with little resistance when you feel overwhelmed.

Remember you are not your emotions

To start with, remembering that who you are is always bigger than your moods ('figure and ground') will prevent you from being swallowed by them. The way we express our emotions in the English language is not always helpful. When we say, 'I am angry' or 'I am sad' it is as though we are fused with that emotion and become one with it. But you are not your emotions, you are the person noticing, noting, observing and witnessing them. Your feelings feel real but are not the truth. They do not define you, bind you or hold you down in any way. Emotions go through your system, but you are not 'in them'. Who you are is much bigger than any thought, feeling or sensation that you have at any given moment. The way to attend to your feelings is not via immersion or identification, but to watch them like drama on a television show. To establish a healthy distance from your emotions, start by changing how you talk to yourself using the following:

- 'I am noticing feelings of anger.'
- 'I can see fear coming my way.'
- 'I realize that sadness is going through me.'
- 'I can acknowledge the feeling of anxiety at the moment.'
- 'I can tell that shame is creating a sinking feeling in my body right now.'

The following visual metaphors are often useful in shifting the figure-and-ground relationship between your sense of self and your feelings:

- Imagine that you are the sky, and the emotions are passing clouds.
- Just as when you are standing at the train station, you do not have to get on every train you see. If the emotions will not take you to the destinations you want, you can just let them pass.
- Think of yourself as the deep, still ocean, and the emotions are waves. No matter how turbulent it is on the surface, you reside within the stillness on the ocean bed.

Feel into your body

Getting to know how your emotions operate in your body will help you to remain engaged but not merged with them. To remind yourself of the transient nature of an emotion, you can learn to notice its fluid nature. Emotions are not static 'things', but moving energy. They are never still, but always emerging as new shapes, sensations and sounds. As you acknowledge their presence in you, they are already on their way out.

As a feeling goes through you, ask yourself the following questions:

- Where does it generate sensations in my body? (It is okay if your body feels numb. You can attend to the numbness in the same way, without trying to change it.)
- Does it move around, or has it found a home in one of your organs, or muscles?
- Does this sensation feel warm or cold?
- If it had a texture, would it be soft or hard?
- If it was made of a material, what would it be? Plastic, metal or wood?
- If it had a colour, what colour would it be?
- Is it static or ever-changing?
- Is it contracting or expanding?
- If it was a painful emotion, how would you describe the quality of this pain? Is it stabbing, throbbing, pulsating, shooting, dull or sharp?

Take the wider view

Looking at our triggers and the emotions themselves from a wider perspective can automatically change how we relate to them. When unpleasant events first happen they always seem exceedingly significant to us, but when we zoom out and look from the outside, we see how brief and insignificant our concerns are. As Stoic philosopher Marcus Aurelius says: 'Everything you see changes in a moment and will soon be gone. Keep in mind always how many of these changes you have already seen' (*Meditations*, 4.3.4).

When you are experiencing a painful emotion, expand your perspective across time and space. Contemplate your entire life stretched out on a timeline, and how transient this moment is in comparison. Imagine rising above the clouds, visualize how small you are as one person in the world and in the grand scheme of the universe.

As a mental note, you may say to or ask yourself the following:

- 'A passing feeling does not define me, who I am is much vaster than this.'
- 'No matter how awful, angry, frightened or fearful I feel now, it will pass.'
- 'Regardless of what is happening inside of me, the world will go on as it always does.'
- 'I am not the only one experiencing this. Somewhere, someone else will be having the exact same feeling.'
- 'Ten years from now, when I look back, how will I feel about what is happening today?'

Talk to your feelings

Your emotions are not your enemies, but messengers sent to you from the depth of your psyche. They are here to tell you something you need to know or prompt an action you need to take. For example, anger is there to tell you your boundaries have been crossed. Anxiety reminds you of what matters to you and prompts you to take action. Sadness helps you to release your armour and get you back in touch with your tender heart. You may not welcome these messengers, but you can have reverence for them. As in all conflict resolution, you can sit down to have a peaceful negotiation with your feelings. When a feeling emerges, slow down your breathing, make some space, and initiate a conversation with it.

Imagine that your feeling is a person. Are they a boy, a girl, a man, a woman, or an androgynous wild spirit that refuses to be defined? Visualize what they look like. What outfit are they wearing? What kind of facial expressions do they have? Approach this person with patience, curiosity and acceptance, and with the intention of 'being with'. You want to get to know their true name; gently ask, 'What is your name? Are you Anxiety? Sadness? Fear? Grief?'

You may ask them the following questions:

- 'What have I overlooked that you are trying to tell me?'
- 'Have my boundaries been compromised in some way?'
- 'Is there something that I need to work through from the past?'
- 'What are you telling me that I need to do for the future?'
- 'Is there any unfinished business with someone close to me?'
- 'Should I go inside and seek solitude, or look outward for external support?'
- 'Is there room for me to be kinder and more generous in my judgement of myself and others?'
- 'What is the one small thing I can do right now that will be useful to the situation?'

When you are done, you can thank your feelings for the messages they have brought you. Be assured that you have got the information you need. You can hold onto the lessons but let go of the feelings. Since the feelings have fulfilled their functions, they may just leave your system with little resistance.

Hands off the control wheel

In their raw form, each emotion comes as a wave but does not last very long. Brain researchers have proposed that the physiological experience of an emotion dissipates within 90 seconds if we do not refuel it with our mind's story.[10] The more you try to 'make sense of', challenge and get rid of an emotion, you refuel the narrative that is recreating it. By doing so, you inflict the same feelings on yourself by pulling the triggers again and again.

When a painful feeling rises in you, you are invited by life to relinquish any preferences of how things 'should be', let go of the expectation to 'feel good', and face the very reality that is here. Think of the reactions to your emotions as a muddy swamp. Like in quicksand, the more you try to escape it, the more stuck you get. Reactive and agitated movements will not only get you sucked in deeper, but your movement will also expand the size of the swamp, making it even harder to reach the solid ground around it. To get out, use slowness, stillness and patient watchfulness. This is not non-action or ridding yourself of responsibility, but taking a wise stance with your actions. If you are brave enough to take your hands off the steering wheel, you will be pleasantly surprised by how the dust always settles after a storm.

Embrace the full spectrum

Despite the hedonistic nature of mainstream culture, making 'happiness' our primary goal in life will only lead to a constant cycle of effort and disappointment. Happiness is a transient state, and life can never go completely the way we want it. As the Buddha holds it, things always change, some pain and loss are inevitable.

Your emotional life is like a flowing river. A stream that is healthy and alive runs as nature intended; it hits the bank on the left and on the right. If you cling only to one dimension – one side of the river – the watercourse will get blocked, flooded and eventually die out. Pleasant and unpleasant feelings are like everything else in nature, you cannot have one without the other – beauty and terror, long and short, high and low, masculine and feminine, breathing in and breathing out. They create each other, shape each other, define each other, complete each other and balance each other. A way of life where we only chase the light and discard the darkness is unsustainable. For example, if you fixate on only wanting happiness, the search for endless sensual pleasure might end up trapping you in an addictive cycle. If you focus on only wanting peace, you might find relationships so messy and unpredictable that you end up living in a lonely void. If you only want what you regard as 'good' and reject, resist or bypass the rest, you will eventually feel nothing but numb and disconnected. The opposite of joy is not pain, but a sore emptiness where you watch life go by without being in it.

As much as you can, loosen your judgement and release the need to label things as 'good or bad'. In truth, emotions are neither positive nor negative; each comes with their unique qualities, functions, guidance and healing opportunities. Take anger, for example; a relationship is invigorated and authentic when differences are allowed, frustrations are aired, and conflicts are released in a healthy and mature way. Anger does not cancel love but can be a part of it.

> Anger and love do not work against each other; they are a complementary part of the whole.

Rather than hiding from your feelings or constantly trying to bend reality the way you want it, a more worthy endeavour is to expand your 'window of tolerance' for different circumstances. You may not enjoy all aspects of your experience, but you can practise staying open to them. When you can find your centre even amidst a range of emotional intensities, you will also find the joy of feeling truly alive.

The answer to the question posed by this chapter's title 'Should you control your emotions?' is a paradox. Essentially, the more you try to control your emotions, the more you will feel out of control. The more you label and judge emotions, the more they haunt you. Whatever you shame, deny and push away will get worse. Paradoxically, however, when you release your need to have things your way, you gain an equanimous 'control' that is not dependent on external circumstances. You can be like a tree that has deep roots in the soil. Although the wind may sway you left and right, back and forth, you will bend but not break. When the storm is over, you remain untethered.

Just like water being carried downstream or a cloud effortlessly floating in the sky, with no resistance, there is no suffering. With no fighting, there are no calamities. You can observe everything and be defined by none. In this journey, I hope you can let go of the demand on yourself to be 'happy', but rather find peace and joy within the complexity of your rich inner world.

Practical strategies: when you are triggered

You may find that certain situations, people or events trigger particularly strong feelings in you, to the point where you lose control of how you feel and react. On the surface, your reactions to these triggers can seem out of proportion. You may get a sinking feeling in your stomach, blow up in rage, crumble with fear or recoil in shame. When your triggers hit you, you flip from being 'normal' one minute to feeling and acting like a completely different person the next, as though there are different personalities inside you. One moment you are active and impulsive, the next moment you are numb, detached and shut down. When you are in a destructive mood, the healthier, resourceful part of you is nowhere to be seen; no logic and reason can bring you back to calm. What makes it even more difficult is that sometimes you don't know the triggers for your emotional flips. You may simply 'wake up feeling bad' without knowing why. Each person's triggers are different. You may be especially sensitive to signs of rejection, humiliation, criticism, abandonment, exclusion … the list is endless, and they relate to your unique experience.

When your reaction seems 'illogical' or 'disproportionate', the real stimulus is almost always an unconscious memory. Your triggers are keys to a frozen memory drawer, in which all the upsetting or overwhelming memories are stored. In this locked-up place, there are not only visual, but also auditory, bodily and feeling memories. For example, you may see the vivid image of your childhood bedroom, or a scene of your parents fighting. You may hear the voice of an inner critic that harshly criticizes you, or have intrusive thoughts such as 'I am no good' or 'I am not safe'. You may experience physical discomfort such as a knot in the stomach, nausea or tightness in the chest. Even without the ability to name them, you get a strong sense that 'the world is a dangerous place' or 'I cannot trust anyone'. When the floodgate opens, you feel and hear all these things as vividly and piercingly as you would as a vulnerable child.

Like many people, you may shame or condemn yourself for having an emotional reaction, especially when its expression is not welcomed by social norms, such as anger or jealousy. A part of you believes that if you harshly scrutinize yourself, you will get better at controlling your feelings. This results in what the Buddhists call 'the second arrow'. The first arrow is the emotion you feel, and the second arrow is your judgement, condemnation or resistance against this feeling. As you add further injury to the original pain, you may just end up in a loop of depression, feeling anxious about your anxiety, or in a downward shame spiral.

Self-condemnation does the exact opposite of helping you flourish. Numerous research studies have found that being self-critical lowers resilience and takes you further away from who you want to be. When your inner critic makes you feel inadequate and insecure, you are more likely to self-sabotage, get paralysed by inaction or lash out at others. In contrast, research has found that self-compassion helps you to be more resilient, reach your goals, have good relationships and perform better at work. With the capacity to regard yourself and your feelings compassionately, you will feel less of a need to compare yourself with or seek approval from others;[11] you can find your internal compass and take actions that align with your values. With repeated practice, you can recondition your brain to respond to emotional triggers not with reactivity, but with self-acceptance and kindness. Although you may still be triggered by events in your life, you can remain anchored by your inner resources until the storm passes.

When an emotional trigger hits you, the first step is to steady your composure, so you do not let one emotion consume the whole of you, or resort to knee-jerk reactions that you might regret later. The following strategies allow you to create some space between the stimulus and response, and to cultivate self-friendliness that will eventually bring resilience.

Pause and attend

Just as you feel a strong feeling emerging in you, slow down, take ten deep breaths and, if you can, retreat to a quiet space, such as your bedroom or bathroom. In whatever way you can, buy yourself a few minutes to conduct this exercise before re-engaging with the outside world.

Start by asking yourself:

- 'Who in me is hurting?'
- 'How old do I feel right now?'
- 'What is the need that has not been met?'

When you 'over-react', it is not the adult you that is behaving badly, but a hurting child. Therefore, as much as you can, approach yourself gently and tenderly, as you would with a wounded young person. Try not to add a 'second arrow' of judgement and condemnation to the suffering. Remind yourself that it is human to feel. You are not the only person who feels this way, and there might be someone out there experiencing the same feeling at that very moment.

Take a moment to acknowledge the feeling that is there. You didn't ask for it, but there it is. Instead of resisting how you feel, consciously name it and greet its arrival like you would with a house guest. You may gently note it in your mind: 'Anger is here', or 'That familiar feeling of shame is coming'. You do not need to pressure yourself to like or 'accept' your feelings. You may even say to yourself: 'I do not like this, I did not ask for this, but I can deal with it for a while'. Remember that the goal of turning towards your feelings is not to make them go away, but to remain steady whilst the storm passes in its own time.

Now, locate the feeling in your body – where do you feel tension? It may be a sinking feeling in your stomach, tension in your shoulder, a lump in your throat. Breathe in and see if you can identify the details of this sensation. Is it light or heavy? Static or shifting? Is the sensation throbbing, pulsating, pounding, beating, dulling or lingering?

Then, imagine holding each one of your feelings in your hands. You are not the fear/anger/panic/envy you are holding, but the person who is looking at them. The feelings do not take over who you are.

Self-friendliness

Now, take a few deep breaths, then bring into your mind a moment when you felt held, loved and soothed by another person. This can also be a spiritual being, an imaginary character, a deceased person, a therapist or a pet. In a moment of struggle for you, they might simply have offered their quiet presence, a gentle tap on your shoulder or a warm hug. Imagine them validating your feelings by saying, 'Of course you can be upset', 'You are allowed to be angry' or 'I am sorry that no one was here for you before'. Imagine seeing yourself through their eyes and, as much as you can, internalize the love, acceptance and compassion they have for you. Imagine them listening to you empathically and understandingly.

Now, transfer the warm and tender feelings into your hands, filling them with healing energy. Slowly and gently, place your palms on your cheeks and allow them to gently rest there. Feel the temperature and texture of your hands, and allow the feeling to sink in. Think about streams of warmth and compassion flowing from your palms into your body, and gradually permeating from your face and head.

Slowly caress your forehead and nose and glide your hands down over your neck and shoulders. If you experience resistance and tension as you move through certain parts, pause and allow your palms to rest there. Your tension may ease, but you do not have to force it to.

Take as long as you wish for this exercise. When you feel ready to, simply rest your palms on your abdominal area. Continue to breath softly and deeply, infusing a sense of ease into the rest of your body.

Although you cannot go back in time to alter the event that caused the triggers in the first place, you can change the physiological association of your memories. Harnessing the power of neuroplasticity, you will gradually heal your deeper wounds and release some emotional changes that come with the triggers.

You can do the above exercise as many times as you need or want to, until an attitude of self-friendliness becomes a default reaction whenever challenging emotions arise.

5

Your relationship with your family

Being intense can be a blessed curse. Because of your intensely sensitive radar, you also pick up more cues from your surroundings. You see what others do not see, including all the hypocrisies and lies. You may not have the language to name it, but you see and absorb the toxic dynamics, unspoken anger and envy in your home environment. As the tale told in Alice Miller's *The Drama of the Gifted Child*, when you are intuitive and empathic, you can become trapped in family patterns in which your gifts are misused or exploited.[1] Before you know it, you may have become the family's emotional caretaker – or worse – emotional sponge, scapegoat or punch bag.

Some parents are emotionally limited. Due to immaturity or trauma, they are unable to love their children the way they need to be loved. Mature parents show their children consistent love and attention, are emotionally open, and allow their children to play and make mistakes. They model resilience, temperance, empathy and compassion. In a precarious world, they act as their children's anchor, or 'secure base', somewhere they can come back to for comfort and reassurance.[2]

In contrast, emotionally inadequate parents may be punitive, unstable, controlling and unable to separate their projections, desires and wishes from their children's life. They are not 'bad people', but children living in adult bodies. They may do their best but still be unable to offer you what you need.

Seeing toxic family dynamics

Our society recognizes the horror of physical child abuse, but not the invisible pain that comes from toxic family patterns. These invisible wounds, however, cut deep. Often, it is not what was said, but what was not said that hurts – the positive feedback, encouragement and affirmations. It is not what was there, but what was not there: quality time, patience, intellectual stimulation, meaningful conversations, family rituals, time for play and humour. There might not be any explicit trauma, but as a result of emotional deprivation, you do not feel welcome in the world. Being stuck in a toxic family situation, your wounds can remain unnoticed for years. You might have been angry, but you could only suppress it. You might have been depressed, but you could only forget how you feel and move on as a mini-adult. However, this kind of trauma does not disappear on its own. The silent scream inside you continues to yell.

> The truth hurts, but a toxic lie kills most silently and insidiously. Self-awareness is the first step to waking up.

The goal of this work is to help you not to be stuck in anger or resentment, but to face up to the truth, and take one leap towards liberation. With this in mind, we will review some toxic family dynamics that commonly entangle a sensitive and intense person.

You are the emotional sponge

Neurologists have found that with the activity of mirror neurons in our brain, we naturally become attuned to other people's emotions. Once we have detected what others feel, we feel compelled to help out. For instance, when we see someone is down, we want to provide comfort and support.[3] This mirror neuron activity becomes amplified when it comes to those who are related to us.[4] Mothers, for example, instinctively mirror their baby's expressions, join them in their laughter and help them calm down when they are distressed.[5]

When we attempt to help another person regulate their emotions – either by cheering them up or calming them down – we are doing what psychologists call 'extrinsic interpersonal emotional regulation'.[6] When you are hyper-empathic, you engage in a lot of 'extrinsic interpersonal emotional regulation' without knowing it. As you enter a space, you immediately pick up the interpersonal signals people are sending but are not verbalizing. Without thinking, you do what you need to do to balance the emotional dynamics. For example, when you sense energy is low in others, you will make a joke, make a scene, use self-deprecating humour, or put yourself in the 'class clown' role to cheer them up. When you detect stress in the home, you park away your own anxiety, put on a brave face, and become the calm anchor everyone else counts on. When you predict the storm of an outburst coming, you know to tuck away your own needs and protect your siblings from harm. When you see your parents sinking into depression, you help around the house or try to elevate their mood. Inadvertently, you are being used by the family to balance what is out of balance, to digest the trauma that is too daunting for their psyche, and to express the unnamed anger. In the long run, you take on the role of being the 'emotional regulator' for the whole family.

On some occasions, you take a step further than being the regulator, and become the 'sponge' for your family's anger, shame, self-pity, and other unwanted emotions. If your parents and siblings have emotional baggage that they were unable to process, they sometimes project it outward and make it your burden. It may surprise you to learn that this can happen, but people do indeed force others to process their unwanted emotions for them. In psychoanalytic psychology, this is called 'projective identification'.

Projective identification is an unconscious mental strategy in which a person discharges feelings and qualities that they reject in themselves onto (and into) other people. When one or more of your family members is wrestling with an emotion that frightens or repel them – such as helplessness, envy or self-hate – they will do all they can to disown that part of themselves. They then lodge it into you and make you experience what they feel deep down, but reject. You, as the recipient, are not aware of this manoeuvre, and think it is 'just you'. For example, your sibling who has deep shame may 'split off' that part of herself and dump it on you. She assumes a superior and dominant position, and makes you feel inferior by talking down at you or bullying you. She has now made you digest her shame for her. Your parents can also project their self-hate and insecurities into you in this way, and have you then carry the burdens of low self-esteem and shame that were never yours to begin with.

Projective identification is more detrimental than a mere 'projection' because it eats into your identity. This mechanism forces you to absorb and take in what has been dumped into your psyche and erodes your sense of self.[7] Projective identification is a severe boundary violation through which your mind and body are infiltrated. Through direct or subtle manipulation, the projections provoke in you an emotional response that brings out genuine identity confusion – you see the shame and hate as coming from you and no longer realize they come from the outside. 'It is as though suddenly you are taken over by thoughts and feelings that are not your own.'[8] Due to your more permeable energy boundaries, being highly sensitive and empathic means you are particularly vulnerable to such violation.

Projective identification happens on an unconscious, right brain to right brain level. Your family members are acting from a desperate, underdeveloped part of themselves, and they are not conscious of what they are doing. At the same time, you could have been the target all your life without knowing it.

Seeing this dynamic is a daunting task. It challenges your worldview at a fundamental level. The part of you that remains protective of your family feels guilty and wants to stay in denial; the part of you that is used to self-blame is frightened of the power that waking up may bring. But if you are brave enough to see what is going on behind the scenes in your family dynamic, you can heal and grow from it.

As a child, you were voiceless, but you now have the power
to say no.

You can set boundaries and physically distance yourself but, more importantly, you can psychologically refuse to take in toxic projections, and reclaim your true self.

Having needy or intrusive parents

Babies have a natural symbiotic relationship with their mothers at birth.[9] At some point, however, they must separate from their parents, and forge their own paths. This is a developmental task for not only the child, but also the parents, who must learn to let go and contain their anxiety.

If your parents have unprocessed trauma, or are emotionally immature, they may feel rejected or abandoned by your need to separate, and they let their emotional hunger override your need to grow. Needy parents intrude on your boundaries because they relate to you not as a separate person, but more like a possession or an extension of themselves. Their behaviours hamper your ability to become independent in these different ways:

- They are over-concerned or over-protective, but the rules they try to enforce come from their anxiety rather than your needs.
- They infantilize you by talking to you in a patronizing or phoney manner.[10] Or, they put you in a 'sick role',

emphasize your incompetence, or portray you to be much less capable than you actually are.

- They act as though you are a part of them, such as speaking for you, going through your belongings, barging into your room or making big and small decisions on your behalf.
- They make you play, perform, or pose for pictures regardless of how you were feeling, and do not leave you alone when you need to be.
- They exert strict rules around the house on orderliness, then insist on cleaning up after you or punish you when you don't comply.
- They are discontent with their lives and live vicariously through you. Since they see you as a direct representation of them, they have an excessive focus on your appearance and achievements.
- They want to be your best friend, confidant, and treat you as theirs by oversharing and relating to you as though you were their partner, not their child. You feel guilty when you make a new friend, don't spend time with them, or share less of your life with them.
- They don't set any boundaries, even when as a child you could benefit from some. They are afraid of conflicts and therefore never modelled discipline or assertiveness for you.

Anxious parents convey the messages: 'Don't go', 'You can't go', 'I cannot survive without you', 'Don't grow up', 'The world is a dangerous place', or even 'You cannot make it on your own'. Behind their need to control is often their fear of not being needed. They may be dissatisfied with their own lives or marriage, and use their children as a way of filling the inner void.

A significant impact of having needy and intrusive parents is the erosion of your self-identity and sense of self-agency. In terms of object relations theory – a branch of psychoanalysis that closely examines how your primary relationships shape your personality, your parents' selfish need to have a merged identity with you will hinder the necessary separation-individuation process.[11] To meet your parents' need to be needed by you, you may have tailored your personality to involve a false sense of dependency. It looks as though you are the debilitated one when, in fact, you have been 'trained' to be needy. You shrink your sense of being and identity smaller and smaller, to the point of being invisible, so you can maintain an indivisible attachment with your parents – which is what they unconsciously want.[12] In other words, the dynamic is set up at home – you are trained to discount your own capability, hold yourself back from independence, and sabotage your success, all without consciously doing so.

Your parents' inability to separate creates an 'enmeshed' family dynamic, in which healthy boundaries are lacking. In enmeshment, you are trained to be intensely affected by, to the point of feeling responsible for, other people's feelings. Having grown up in an enmeshed family, you may now struggle to tell the difference between your own emotions and those around you, to not take on others' projections, or to say no to an excessive demand. The psychic merger with your parents may look like genuine closeness, but the two are very different. In a healthy, loving relationship, you retain a sense of self and feel free to come and go. In enmeshment, you are suffocated. You may not consciously feel you want to sacrifice your life for your unhappy parents, but just like a fish does not know water, you have lived all your life on a rescue mission that you are not aware you were on. If you pay close attention, you will realize that, when you are in their presence, there is a subtle energetic pull through which your body is pulled in and weighed down.

Your parents were the only people you depended on as a child, and you did not have the liberty to escape, nor language to stand up for yourself. If one or both of your parents did not respect your boundaries, the violation would have left a strong imprint on your psyche. These intrusions can bring about what psychoanalysts call annihilation anxieties – the terror of completely losing oneself, of ceasing to exist. The fear of annihilation can be broken down into the following dimensions:

- Fears of being overwhelmed, being unable to cope, and of losing control
- Fears of merger, entrapment, or being devoured
- Fears of the disintegration of self or of identity, of meaninglessness, or nothingness, or of humiliation-mortification
- Fears of impingement, penetration, or mutilation
- Fears of abandonment or need for support
- Apprehensions over survival, persecution, catastrophe.[13]

Annihilation anxieties can turn into the fear of abandonment and engulfment, and affect how you relate to people in your future relationship. You may have conditions such as panic, nightmares, phobias, dissociation and other physical symptoms without knowing their links to your experience of early intrusions.

Rather than it being a malicious manoeuvre on the parents' part, intrusion is a result of unprocessed traumatic family patterns being passed down trans-generationally. They do not realize what they are doing, but they are acting out from their hunger for attachment. However, that does not mean it is your job to fix things or to heal their wounds.

On a deep level, they know their childlike ways are detrimental to both their own and your growth, however, given it is such an entrenched pattern they do not know how to change it. If your parents are emotionally needy and don't know where to draw the line, you have to take the lead and set an example of healthy boundaries. Even if this is unwelcome at first, it is ultimately the best for you, for them, and those around you.

You were overburdened and 'parentified'

Parentification is when the roles are reversed between a child and a parent, where the child has to take up responsibilities that rightfully belong to the adults. It is a toxic family dynamic that is rarely discussed, often shielded under the name of love, loyalty, filial piety and indeed accepted as the norm in some cultures. However, research has found that it can have far-reaching psychological impacts.[14]

There are two types of parentification:

- Instrumental parentification is when you take care of tasks such as housework, cooking and cleaning too much and too soon in your life. You may have to take care of your own physical needs, such as going to the doctor on your own.
- Emotional parentification is when you become your parents' counsellor, confidant, or emotional caretaker, or the family mediator.

In this dynamic, the roles in the family were reversed in childhood because it was not safe for you to bring your child-self out. The innocent spirit in you was stifled as you had to grow up quickly. If you had brought your vulnerable child out to your parents, hoping and yearning for care, you would have been disappointed, traumatized and hurt. So, from the get-go, you learned that the only safe thing to do was to rise above your pain and to hide your vulnerability.

Emotional parentification sometimes involves 'emotional incest', where the child is treated as an intimate partner to the parent. Perhaps one of them is unhappy in their own marriage or dissatisfied with their lives. They overshare their feelings and frustration with their child, cry, complain or even hurt themselves in front of them. The child then feels responsible to alleviate their suffering, even though what they share is too heavy for a young psyche to handle.

Alongside taking care of your parents, you may also have to stand in as your siblings' parents. As a result, you feel tremendous guilt when you have to leave at some point – for instance, for college. You may feel as though you were abandoning your own children.

Parentification is often punctuated by horrific tasks, such as preventing an addicted parent from overdosing, or protecting siblings from violent outbursts. As a highly sensitive and intuitive child, perhaps you were the first one to detect these unsafe and unstable conditions, and now you take it upon yourself to provide care and support for the family. This may have led to an overwhelming sense of anxiety about the needs and feelings of others and put you in a hypervigilant state that, even as adult, you are unable to return from.

Regardless of how mature you might have been or acted, you were only a child. All children are, by default, helpless and dependent on their caregiver. They need a guardian in this unknown and sometimes scary and dangerous world. But with no one to look up to, to lean on, or to receive guidance from, you were left in a state of insecurity.

It was never possible for you to cure your parents of their own pain, but because it felt like your responsibility, you end up with a chronic feeling that you are falling short. Even as an adult, you have an overdeveloped sense of responsibility in relationships. You may overinvest in friendships and relationships, blame yourself for things that go wrong, or attract partners that take more than they give. In the long run, these patterns could lead to physical and emotional fatigue, and the desire to shut down completely.

What makes the situation challenging is that it is very difficult for you to be angry at your parents. Often, they do not present as abusive, but helpless and vulnerable. Since you were endowed with compassion and maturity beyond your age, you felt compelled to help, and your protective instinct holds you back from acknowledging the truth of what was lacking for you.

You might have been a skilled parent figure to others all your lives, but now it is time for you to parent yourself.

> The goal of healing is to start prioritizing your needs before you jump into pleasing others.

As a child, you needed love, attention, and to be heard. You also needed room to play, make a mess, and explore the world – without being burdened with responsibilities. If you were deprived of these in the past, it is now within your power to reclaim your lost childhood.

You were oppressed by a competitive parent

Although it is a taboo subject in society, it is natural to have mixed feelings about parenting.[15] The fact that parents want the best for their children does not negate the frustration and even hostility they sometimes feel. In particular, it is not uncommon for them to be jealous of their children. As your parents age, they can bereave over their unfulfilled lives, which makes it difficult for them to witness you getting the resources and opportunities they had wanted for themselves. If they are resentful towards the time and energy they have given up for parenthood, they may feel betrayed when you leave the nest. They may also regress psychologically and start seeing you as a rival. They become threatened by the prospect of you becoming more successful, beautiful, or competent than they are. Healthy parents can acknowledge their complicated feelings, but emotionally immature parents act them out in such ways as giving back-handed compliments, subtle put-downs, or by explicit contempt and scorn.

If you were a gifted child and your parents had unfulfilled lives, their ability to be wholeheartedly supportive of your emergence may have been constrained. Not only did they not have the intellectual capacity to comprehend your gifts, they also failed to serve as robust role models. Due to rapid changes in women's rights throughout the last few decades, this can be especially challenging for mothers. On the surface, she encourages you to succeed, but her life choices convey the messages that to be a woman means to make compromises, to give up one's dreams, and to settle for less.[16] When you emerge as a strong and independent woman, you call into question the meaning of your mother's life, provoking conflict or covert anger.

Children look up to their parents – especially the parent of the same gender. If your role model punishes you for your accomplishments, you may eventually internalize the disdain as self-hatred and low self-esteem. The messages of oppression might be buried deep in the unconscious, but whenever you do well in life, you feel inexplicable guilt or shame. You feel like an imposter, so you sabotage your success. To stay safe, you play small.

While this does not excuse their behaviours, competitive parents are also victims of deprivation in their childhood. As they have not experienced unconditional positive regards for their own flourishing in life, they are unable to then give it.

You are scapegoated and gaslighted

Healthy families honour and celebrate individual differences; dysfunctional families, in contrast, have little tolerance for idiosyncrasies. Andrew Solomon, who conducted over 4000 interviews with families in his book *Far from the Tree*, observed that having exceptional children exaggerates parental tendencies; those who would be bad parents become awful parents, but those who would be good parents become extraordinary.[17]

Unfortunately, in many of the former cases, the one who is different becomes the scapegoat.

Pointing the finger at one person as the cause of all evil is an unconscious strategy used by families to evade their own emotional pain. It is 'unconsciously intentional'. Once the pattern is set, the family typically goes to great lengths to keep the dynamic that way. The scapegoat must remain the scapegoat. When the scapegoat tries to walk away from this toxic dynamic, they are met with subtle or not-so-subtle emotional revenge, or threats of abandonment.

Here are some of the signs that you have been scapegoated in your family:

- You are criticized for your natural attributes, such as being intense and sensitive.
- Your achievements are never praised or valued, but ignored, dismissed or belittled.
- You are blamed for bad things that happen to or in the family.
- You feel invisible; your family does not seem interested in getting to know the real you.
- Your mistakes are blown out of proportion or punished disproportionately.
- Your family portray you in a negative light to others.
- Your family boycotts you in family activities, or holds family secrets away from you.
- Name calling – you are always 'the weird one', the 'wild card', or 'the trouble'.

When you thrive, get stronger and more independent, you sense your family's intent to bring you down. Scapegoating often goes alongside gaslighting, a strategy that is designed to dilute your voice and cover up the truth. In gaslighting, your family acts as a group to sow seeds of doubt in you, making you question what you see, think, feel and remember. Theorists of systemic family therapy use the term 'identified patient' to describe the scapegoated person, because they are made to feel like the 'patient' whose sanity is in question.[18]

Through tactics such as denial, deflection and even blatant lies, your family group delegitimizes what you have to say. For example, when you try to talk about your experience in the family, you are told that you imagined it. You are repeatedly told: 'Nothing bad has happened to you', 'We are a happy family', 'No one else but you remember these bad events'. When these false narratives are presented to you all your life, it becomes impossible to go against the grain. Eventually you stop trusting yourself. You may become someone who runs on empty, devoid of your own thoughts, feelings and convictions, and live in a confused, half-dissociated state.

To heal from scapegoating and gaslighting takes time. You may intellectually understand that you are not the cause of problems in your family, but to shift the internalized shame requires more profound emotional healing. You must realize that the cause of chaos is not you, but your family's repressed baggage, and it should never have been your responsibility as a child to carry any burden that is not yours.

Personality adaptations

For better or for worse, your early family experience is formative of who you are today. As a child, you had to find ways of thinking and behaving that would allow you to make sense of what happened. What started as a means to survive a painful childhood then forms a big part of your personality – sometimes affecting you for life. Here are some common personality adaptation patterns resulting from a difficult childhood:

- If your parents tended to praise you only for what you did and not who you were, you would have learned to see your own worth based on external achievements. Rather than allowing yourself to just 'be', you become a 'human doing'. The only way you know to survive in the world is to work hard, to achieve the next credential, and to never slow down. You live according to metrics and standards set by society, rather than your true spontaneous self. This pattern leaves you feeling empty on the inside and, from time to time, you wonder if you are acceptable without something impressive to show.

- If your parents were depressed and relied on you for love and comfort, you might have learned to define yourself through the eyes of others. You feel as though the centre of gravity lies in other people and not in yourself. While you are highly empathic and attuned to people's needs, you lose touch with your own needs. You feel you are constantly trying to earn love from those around you. No matter how helpful and loving you are, people do not seem to reciprocate to the same degree. When they don't, it hurts deeply.

- If you were overburdened with responsibilities as a child, you may have become highly sensitized to errors, imperfection and unfairness in the world. You hear the voice of a harsh inner critic, who constantly tells you that things are not done correctly or perfectly enough. You live with constant pressure to fix things. Being highly judgemental and critical also come between you and those you love. You didn't mean to, but those around you feel scrutinized and pressured.

- If your childhood environment was unstable and unsafe, you would have been deprived of the opportunity to cultivate trust in the universe. Doubt and fears become your default. Always vigilant and watchful, you never stop scanning the environment for threats. You are often held in 'analysis-paralysis', making a long list of 'what might go wrong' rather than taking productive action. Your diligence may protect you, but your fears stop you from reaching your potential.

- If your parents have emotionally or physically abandoned you, you may, for your whole life, feel like an orphan on the inside. You feel misunderstood and unable to fit in wherever you go. Your inner critic derails your self-esteem by comparing you to others, telling you they all have a happier, more 'normal' and fulfilling life. Over time, depression and envy take over and cut you off from contentment.

- If your parents were bullies, you would have learned early in your life to survive on power and assertion. You see the world as a dog-eat-dog place, and it is risky to let your guard down. It becomes impossible to reveal your vulnerabilities to anyone, or to let people in to help and comfort you. You have put up a wall to keep you safe, but it also keeps you in isolation. Even when you have achieved power in the world, you feel incredibly alone.

Because the ways you have adapted to survive are unique to you, the pathway you will take towards healing is also unique. Through a process of careful examination and unravelling, you can trace your story back to where it started. You do not have to reject your 'adapted self' who is perfectionist, highly anxious or trapped in people-pleasing. Remember, your protective mechanism is an honourable part of you that has helped you survive in some very difficult times. You can greet it, bow to it, and honour it. As though your survival pattern was a person, you may say to them: 'Thank you for your service, my brave soldier. I know now what to do, and you can relax and rest.'

Addressing the root of your emotional pain marks a critical juncture in the reparative process.

While you cannot go back in time to change the past, it does not have to weigh you down for the rest of your life.

Transcending your past

Reflect on the following about your family:

- Do they know you?
- Do they know the real, intense, gifted, unconventional and unique being that you are?
- Do they understand that you have a unique set of needs because of your sensitivity?
- Do they have the capacity to understand your values and beliefs?
- Do they celebrate your enthusiasm and passion without shutting you down?
- Do they respect and honour your vision or ambition, even when it has gone beyond all their frames of reference?

Perhaps they do, perhaps they don't. Perhaps sometimes they do, sometimes they don't.

Their inability to see, hear and embrace you for who you are hurts. Their opinions and intrusions are humiliating, hurtful, or suffocating.

To thrive means not being held back by your family's expectations, judgement and opinions.

Healing your childhood hurt is an essential path to attaining inner peace. Without transforming your wounds, triggers for unexpected rage, unfounded guilt and shame spirals will always be lurking in the background, catching you off guard; they may sabotage your relationships, block your creativity, and hold you back in life.

'My parents could not, or did not, love me the way I need to be loved.' Acknowledging this painful truth involves you courageously processing emotions such as deep grief, anger and hurt. These feelings are excruciating, but temporary unless you block them. If you know that you are on a path towards liberation, and allow these feelings to go through you, you will be rewarded with freedom at the other end. In the next chapter, we will dive deeper into the process of releasing the past. With practice, you can gradually learn to draw a line between who you are and their projections. You can separate your life choices from the wishes and dreams they did not experience, and say no to them wanting to live vicariously through you. You also have the right to release the compulsive need to caretake, rescue or counsel. You fully deserve to be unconditionally loved for who you are and, regardless of your parents' limitations, you can do that for yourself.

Ultimately, your biological family does not equal your soul's family. Your parents are simply the universe's vessels to bring you into being, and your original family is where you were housed to learn the lessons of individuation, tolerance, forgiveness and wider compassion. You are real, perfect and whole just as you are; those who belong to your true home will see this, embrace this, and celebrate this. Even when your actual childhood may be nauseatingly painful and full of holes, it is never too late to give yourself the childhood that you deserve.

Reflective exercise: looking through the family album

Your family albums are documentaries of your roots and a rich source of information about your family relationships, traditions, values and history. By exploring old family pictures in an attentive and in-depth way, you will unveil surprising patterns and truths that you perhaps were not previously aware of.

Set aside some quiet time for this exercise. Bring out your family albums, or any collection of old family pictures you can find. See if you can find a variety of images, ranging from formal family events such as weddings and parties, snapshots of a few members in the family, to the family travelogues. Spend as much time as you like to look through them, then pick out about 10–20 images that jump out at you.

Lay these images in front of you while you go through the following questions. Write your answers in your journal. Remember, no one needs to see what you have written. This is a private space for you to attend to what was ignored, respect what was dismissed, and to articulate what was silenced. As much as possible, don't let the feelings of guilt, shame or rage stop you from writing; instead, put these feelings on paper and allow them to be expressed and digested.

As you review the images, notice the quality of the connection between each family member.

- Who tends to go to whom for what?
- Are certain family members often captured next to each other?
- Notice the power dynamic, who is in charge most of the time?
- Who expresses the most emotions and who does the opposite?
- Can you tell who took these pictures? What sentiments are expressed by the photographer(s)?
- What emotions are encouraged/discouraged in this family (e.g. 'excitement' is encouraged, 'anger' is discouraged)? Who gets to decide what is acceptable and what is not?
- How are conflicts and disagreements handled? Who gets to decide that?

- What happens when someone makes a mistake or experiences a setback?
- Is there a difference between how your family represents itself to the outside world and what happens behind the scene?
- What was it like to be a child in this family?
- Did the family dynamics change or have they remained the same throughout the years?
- If you could take a person out from these pictures, who would you take out?
- If you could add a person in these pictures, who would you add?

Very often, a family member will carry a particular 'role', which represents recurrent patterns of behaviour by which they fulfil family functions and needs.[19] Now, reflect on who in your family, including yourself, might be the bearers of these roles:

- The Golden Boy/Girl: the high achiever, pride of the family.
- The Leader: the one who holds authority, acts as the organizer, and who everyone counts on to solve problems.
- The Rescuer: the one who takes on others' emotions and problems, jumps in to rescue, and is always busy prioritizing others over their own needs.
- The Peacemaker: the one to keep peace, to act as a buffer when conflict arises between other members.
- The Scapegoat: the one who is blamed for all the bad things that happen.
- The Black Sheep: the one that does not fit in, the misfit, outcast, the 'weird one'.
- The Lost Child: the subservient, obedient, quiet one who is hidden and unnoticed.
- The Clown: the one who acts as a cheerleader and uses their gift of humour to defuse conflicts in the family. Their own true feelings might be hidden.

Review the health of the relationships and boundaries you have with your family, both in the past and as it stands today.

- Who were/are you the closest to?
- Who did/do you feel the most loved by?
- Who did/do you feel the most protective towards?
- Did/do you feel safe with your family?
- Were you/are you in a co-dependent relationship(s) with one or more of your family members?
- Do you feel that you always try to change one or more of your family members?
- Do you feel coerced into certain family rules or rituals?

Notice the assumptions, expectations and manipulations that have been put upon you, maybe all your life, without your consent. Doubts may emerge, but try to trust what you feel beyond appearances and longstanding family myths. You now have the right to release the truths you have recognized about your family.

This exercise may evoke powerful feelings in you. On completion, take a moment to ground yourself. Briefly scan your body, notice any tension and ripples that have come up. Honour all feelings, even when they seem mixed and irrational – sadness, grief, anger, envy, fear, guilt, shame, joy, gratitude. Noticing your feelings and writing your truth is entirely safe. You have not done anything wrong, or harmed anyone. As much as possible, imagine breathing in self-compassion into the tight areas within yourself. If it feels difficult to be generous with yourself, you may bring into mind a person or a child you love, and experience the quality of softness in your heart. Then, see if you can direct these tender feelings towards yourself.

Finally, close your journal, take a moment to reflect on your overall experience, and congratulate yourself for having given yourself the time to heal.

Releasing the past

As you are processing painful wounds from your past, the idea of 'forgiveness' seems daunting. The word itself is loaded, vague and tinted with moralistic associations. In this chapter, we will look at what it means to be free from the trauma of being let down by your early caregivers. Healing from the past involves facing the pain of a childhood where your needs were not met, processing the resentment you may be holding towards your parents, and working out how to navigate ongoing relationships with your family. The goal here is not to harbour self-pity nor to blame anyone, but to validate the pain that is there, so you can work towards letting go of the emotional poisons that are holding you back.

You are releasing the past not for anyone else's sake, not because society has asked you to, but because you ache to be free. Releasing in no way requires you to change, or to trust people who have previously harmed you. This is a quest to free yourself, and it promises many gifts when achieved. Once you have done this for yourself, you will no longer cast past shadows onto your partners, or let rage or unrealistic expectations ruin the love you have. You will loosen the grip on internalized shame, low self-esteem, addictions and compulsions, and you will no longer be compulsively drawn to abusive or imbalanced relationships. You will also free up energy to wholeheartedly pursue your dreams and goals. This chapter presents the process of releasing in five stages. Although they are presented in a linear fashion, in reality they are not separate and chronological. You may experience a few stages at the same time or go back and forth between them.

Step 1: Tell the truth
Step 2: Allow anger to flow through
Step 3: Grieve and reconcile with reality

Step 4: Integrate with compassion
Step 5: Relate with strength

Step 1: Tell the truth

Unveiling what has been buried all your life is an essential first step to releasing it. As a lifelong emotional caretaker of your family, you may minimize and brush off everything you have endured. Whenever someone asks you about the past, your default answer may be 'I had a happy childhood'. When confronted, you jump to rationalizing by saying: 'They did the best they could' or 'Other people have it much worse'. When someone asks you about your parents, you are unable to say anything negative about them. You may even feel guilty for not having been a 'happier' person given that everything on the outside seemed 'fine'. You have few memories of your early years or find yourself hitting a wall of emotional numbness when you search within. Since the trauma you experienced was mostly invisible, you have difficulty acknowledging it. However, turning a blind eye does not make your trauma disappear. Forgiving is not forgetting; in fact, forgetting is the antidote to forgiving. By burying your story and stifling your anger, you cannot achieve anything beyond surface harmony. By prematurely moving into false compassion and spiritual bypass, you are putting a bandage on a wound that will not heal itself, and perpetuating dysfunctional patterns that can be passed down to the next generation.

You may feel as though you cannot afford to retrace your trauma, but the reality is that you cannot afford not to. You must do this for your one and only life. Forgetting might have been what you needed to do to survive so far but, in the long run, it sets a dangerous precedent. When you deny what has happened to you, the trauma becomes lodged in your body in frozen form,[20] forcing you to dissociate from parts of yourself. As you dissociate, you also become more inept at connecting with others and become depressed, stuck in life, in relationships, even in therapy. It will become a self-devouring cycle that keeps you in a state of suspension – not alive but not fully dead. As described by Donald Kalsched in his book *Trauma and the Soul*, a person stuck in such a predicament does not feel completely real and is unable to commit wholeheartedly to anything or anyone.[21] They exist in a limbo, living a 'provisional life'. That inner emptiness is a dreadful soul suicide and is no less devastating than your original trauma.

You may be trapped in denial because of your family's investment in denying the problem. Emotionally inadequate parents feel like they are trying their hardest, but deep down they know they have failed you. Ironically, they then take out their unconscious shame and guilt on you by making you feel like a bad, spoilt person. They may resort to buying excessive material provisions for you, so that from the outside you look as though you are loved. The whole family may portray you as the 'crazy' one. If you dare to let your truth leak out into the world, you are punished for being ungrateful and demanding. But burying your truth only creates a vicious cycle that locks you in co-dependency. Therefore, you must take the step to see the truth, even if it is ugly, painful or unwelcome by those involved.

You can begin this process by questioning the narrative you have followed all your life and allowing your memories to resurface in a safe place. It is a sobering but liberating act, to see that unlike the superman or superwoman your child-self had needed your parents to be, they are wounded and limited human beings. They might have acted out because of their insecurities, projections, trauma and wounds. They did not understand your intensity, felt threatened by your intuition and tried to stifle your voice. You were used to compensating for their un-lived lives, and being the container for the anxiety that they could not bear.

To heal, you do not need to blame anyone, you do not even have to confront your family. You might want to tell your story to one trusted confidant or your therapist, or you can do the work in your private space. For example, try talking to an empty chair, where you can say what needs to be said without consequences. You could write a letter to your parents but not send it, or create a piece of art or music that captures your story. You could even practise what psychologists call imagery rescripting,[22] where you imagine entering your past as a resourceful adult, and stand up for the 'younger you' who was vulnerable and defenceless at the time. The neural network in our brain works in mysterious ways; although you cannot change history, research has found we experience powerful therapeutic effects just by imagining a changed story in our mind.

The first step to releasing is to honour your true story and seek justice where you can. Even if receiving an apology is not possible, you can at least choose to accept the imperfect reality as it is and relieve yourself of the duty to live a lie.

Step 2: Allow anger to flow through

Anger is one of the most challenging elements in the releasing process. Because of our cultural conditioning, you may have been led to believe that anger is 'bad', that it means aggression, or that being angry will alienate you from others. You were trained by authorities and institutions to suppress your anger so that everyone around you felt comfortable. Holding resentment towards our parents is a social taboo, and you now feel guilty or even ashamed of your legitimate rage. You may have spent years suppressing, displacing and contorting it, but now you may find that the more you make demons out of your anger, the more it grows. The more you reject it, the more it sticks.

As a child, admitting that your parents were neglectful or abusive was a life-threatening idea, for they were the only people you could depend on. If you knew your parents would not tolerate a challenge, or that you would be punished for speaking up, of course you would not dare to be critical of the authority figures whose goodwill was essential to your survival. This can result in a psychodynamic process known as 'turning against the self',[23] where a person redirects anger and resentment for others towards themselves. Blaming yourself gave your young mind a sense of control. Rather than accepting how powerless you were or admitting the horror of being stuck with unreliable parents, you found it easier to believe it was you who created the situation. That way, you might be able to fix it — by becoming a better child, or by pleasing them. Self-blame gave you an explanation for the unbearable injustice that had happened and, at that moment, it was more tolerable than the alternative. As psychologist Ronald Fairbairn said, 'It is better to live as a sinner in a world created by God, than to live in a world created by the devil.'[24]

However, turning anger inward is not a sustainable defence mechanism. If you internalize your anger, you can become psychologically, and sometimes physically, violent towards yourself. To release the past, you must stop chasing your own tail. The truth is that anger, like all feelings, is not right or wrong, good or bad. Anger is a natural reaction when someone has violated your values or boundaries. At its core, anger is a cry for help. If you look closely, you will find sadness behind the anger, and deep pain in the sadness that is waiting to be healed and integrated. Anger is a healthy emotion, if you relate to it as such, and it is only destructive when you turn it into a weapon against yourself or others. When harnessed correctly, it propels you to take productive action.

At first, you may feel guilty for giving yourself a voice. You may worry that those you care about will not survive the truth, or that you are betraying a family narrative. However, whatever was the cause of your parents' behaviour, be it their own childhood trauma or personality limitations, it does not negate the pain you have suffered. It was not your job as a child to find excuses for them or to protect them. To mobilize healthy anger, perhaps you can ask yourself: how would you feel if what had happened to you happens to a child you love? If the naked truth were to be presented in court, how would you defend the child's welfare?

There are many ways to process anger; rather than trying to think your way out of it via rationalization, see if you can allow it to move through your body. You can do this through sounds, movements and expressive arts. Start by seeing anger as a form of pure energy and suspending any value judgement on it. By becoming mindful of your body, you can feel the pulsating sensation the anger creates in your cells. Then, imagine yourself as a channel, through which the spirit of anger could come in, get through, and eventually leave your system. If you are not so afraid of releasing it bit by bit, anger will not build up to the point of explosion.

Once you have a healthy relationship with anger, you will witness the following changes:

- When someone hurts you, you will stand up for yourself instead of sinking into depression.
- When something unjust happens in the world, you can turn your fury into energy that propels action.
- When someone crosses your boundaries, you are assertive but not defensive or aggressive.

It is critical that you balance the energy of compassion with some form of healthy anger, otherwise you run the risk of false forgiveness. You cannot jump ahead to forgiving others without first having reverence for the pain you have endured. Healthy anger is the gateway to feeling courage through your body, having clarity in your mind, and being empowered in your spirit. When you see its true nature, you embrace and even cherish it as a vital life force.

Step 3: Grieve and reconcile with reality

Do you sometimes wonder why you are triggered by your parents even when they are old, frail and living far away from you? Even when you have walked away and have your own family, whenever you get in touch with them or visit, you regress and revert to feeling like a five-year-old or a raging teenager. Even in your mind you know you must move forward from the past; you may be stuck in the past, in anger, in resentment, and in constant reactivity.

You are not alone in facing this predicament. It is a part of our human tendency to keep trying to knock on the wrong door to have our needs met, even when the results are repeatedly disappointing. If you carefully examine what you want from an interaction with your parents, you may find it falls into the following categories: attention, comfort, reassurance, appreciation, celebration of your success or achievement. Unconsciously, you still want your parents to meet the emotional needs that were not met in your childhood. From time to time, they seem to give you what you want and so you get lured in by glimpses of hope, but when they once again act in a hurtful way, you regret having tried and the cycle continues. Even if your mind knows you are now an adult, your body holds the visceral memories of having been let down. Therefore, when they disappoint you, it is understandable that you respond with the anger, sadness, grief and fears that belong to a fearful toddler. In psychology, this behavioural loop is called 'repetition compulsion'.

At first glance, grief does not seem to be a relevant emotion, but underlying your repetition compulsion is the refusal to grieve. We normally grieve for something we had and lost but, in this case, you are grieving something you never had – the parents you wanted or the childhood you needed. You are still hoping and yearning for that reality. A part of you still tries to make your parents love you the way you want. Sadly, continuing to seek in them for what they cannot give means you are disappointed over and over without an apology.

By grieving, you are accepting a 'meaningful suffering' that will ultimately liberate you. Jungian analyst Helen Luke likens frozen grief to an inferno: 'as long as we seek to escape from our various "hells", we remain irremediably bound; we can emerge from the pains of hell in one way only – by accepting another kind of suffering, the suffering which is purging, instead of meaningless damnation'.[25] In grieving, you shatter your hopes and dreams for an ideal upbringing. You accept the cold hard truth that you are owed an apology that may never come. You live with the fact that the interactions will never be the way you want them. You reconcile with the possibility that things may never change. Your childhood experience is not just or justified, yet it is the only one you have. Living with reality as it is is always better than trying to change it and being disappointed every time. At first, it feels like accepting defeat, but sometimes in life, to win a war, we must surrender a battle. If you can lose the 'fantasy world' you have been holding onto, you can move to the realm of a rich and solid reality. The cure to your depression is not to replace it with happy feelings, but to solemnly work with what is, so you come out the other end.

After you have fully grieved, you may find it easier to interact with your parents. As long as you are able to manage your expectations, you can even enjoy each other's company. It is by lucidly reckoning with others' limits and coming to terms with their humanity we can enter the realm of love. Grieving for what you never had and accepting your family's dysfunctions will deepen your relationships, not just with them but also everyone around you. Initially, it is excruciating, but if you can work through the pain to heal the gaping hole in your soul, you will be redeemed from the loop of disappointment and despair.

Step 4: Integrate with compassion

Research has shown that lots of trauma is transgenerational. The dysfunctional traits your parents have may come not directly from them but from the wounds they have inherited. In each parent there is, in psychoanalytic terms, an 'introjected bad parent'. They have 'introjected' – absorbed and adopted – the dysfunctional attitude and behaviours of their parents. They may alternate in their behaviours in a 'Jekyll and Hyde' way. They are loving on some days but, in times of stress, their 'introjected bad parents' come out and catch you off guard with rage, coldness and cruelty. A part of your releasing process is learning how to see both the 'good parent' and the 'bad parent' in them. By doing so, you mature into seeing the complexity of humanity: no one, including yourself, is one-dimensional. Even your parents can be a source of both nourishment and disappointment, love and cruelty. Grappling paradoxes would have been impossible to understand with the mental capacity of a child, but it is something you can do now. If you see them not from the perspective of a hurting child but from an understanding adult, you may see how deprived and wounded your parents are, and how helpless they are in the face of their conditioning. They, too, have been traumatized by their parents' neglect, abuse or attacks.

For a moment, reflect on their lives. This exercise could be supplemented with pictures of your parents when they were younger, if you have access to old photographs.

- What did they dream of and aspire to be when they were young?
- How has the cruelty and harshness of humanity disappointed them?
- What has taken away their innocence and trust?

Looking deeply, you may see that:

- If they are highly judgemental, it is because they judge themselves.
- If they are too eager to defend themselves, it is because, deep down, they feel guilty and ashamed of who they are.
- If they blame you for your struggles and unhappiness, it may be because, on some level, they feel they have failed you.
- If you see beyond the surface, you will see the scared children in their psyche.

Recall a time when your parents' behaviours triggered a strong feeling in you, then ask yourself: 'How would I respond if this was a stranger?' See if you can see your parents not as 'your parents' but as fellow human beings who are also on their own paths, struggling with the universal predicaments of life such as death, pain and uncertainty. Then you can generate a kind of 'dispassionate' compassion for them. This form of compassion is another form of love, but one that is not engulfing, does not take away from you, and can be extended to the rest of humankind.

Knowing that your parents are acting out of their inherited wounds, you do not have to take what they say or do personally. You do not have to engage, interact or argue with their accusations. Without you pouring gasoline on the fire, the 'bad parents' in them cannot find a person to be cruel towards, no enemy to engage with, and will gradually cease to appear. This does not mean you are approving, accepting or tolerating abuse; you are simply responding as a dignified adult. Ultimately, by adopting a wider perspective that includes compassion, you are freeing yourself.

Step 5: Relate with strength

Consciously or unconsciously, many of us feel we owe our parents. Somehow, we were led to believe that we should be responsible for their livelihood, wellbeing and happiness later in life. The indebtedness we feel causes us to be in an enmeshed dynamic with them or be stuck in a mission to rescue. You might feel responsible for your parents because they have sacrificed for you, but this can quickly turn into toxic guilt and resentment. The truth is that you cannot coerce yourself into love because of loyalty and filial piety. Genuine compassion comes naturally, without any sense of forced responsibility.

Poet Kahlil Gibran gives some thought-provoking advice on parenting:[26]

'Your children are not your children.

They are the sons and daughters of Life's longing for itself.

They come through you but not from you,

And though they are with you, yet they belong not to you.'

Gibran then likens parents as the bows from which children as living arrows are sent forth. Children have minds that shouldn't be infiltrated by their parents' agenda, and they should not be held hostage to conditional love.

Gibran's prose inspires us to rethink who we are in relation to our parents. People who are religious have always known that they are ultimately 'children of God', but you do not have to be religious to adopt a spiritual perspective. Like everything else, you are a part of nature. Imagine yourself as a tiny seedling that did not come from the physical bodies of your father or mother, but from a universal life source. Like any animal in the wild, or any tree in a forest, you come into being as part of an organic process. Consider the cycles in nature, things are produced but not possessed. Nutrients from the soil, sunshine and rainfall are freely given without needing anything in return. Nature does not want an oak tree to become a pine tree, nor a rose to be a sunflower, but for everything to be what it is meant to be. It honours your individual path and wants you to grow into the most authentic you. However quirky and non-conforming you are, you are deserving of unconditional love and respect.

You do not owe your parents anything, and you are not responsible for their lives. You are a child of nature, and your parents are simply the instruments that brought you into being.

As well as the burden of false responsibilities, you may also be trapped in a loop with your parents because you have unconscious expectations for them to be different. Repeated frustrations stem from your need for your parents to do what you believe is ethical, right or good for them. However, the same way they should not have any control over who you are and the paths you choose, you do not have the right to change them. If we reverse Gibran's words 'your children are not your children', we see that our parents are also not 'our parents'. Just like any stranger we encounter today, they are fellow human beings in this world, with their own personalities and paths in life. You are not responsible for your parents' wellbeing, and you don't have the right to determine what they do with their lives. What seems dysfunctional and limited in your eyes, may be the best they can do; even if not, it is not for you to prescribe remedies for their decisions. Who they are has been determined and decided before your birth, and perhaps even they have little control over it. You can negotiate the terms of your communication, but you cannot change their personalities to suit you. You can control your actions and the efforts you make, but you have little control over whether your parents respond.

Sometimes, to free yourself, you must relinquish the hope that your parents will treat you with the love and respect you need. When you take the plunge and separate from them, they may react with aggression, threats or accusations. They may frame you as a traitor, ungrateful or selfish. The rigidity of their lifelong defence mechanisms prevents them from being truly empathic, authentic and able to see your perspective. They may continue to be overbearing, hysterical and argumentative for the rest of their lives, and there is little you can do about it. It can be excruciating to grapple with, but the reality is that no amount of explanation will gain you justice or fairness. The more time and energy you invest in this losing battle, the further away you move from the life you truly want and deserve.

While apologies and redemption are not always possible, it is in your power to manage your emotional triggers, set boundaries, and healthily relate to your family. With the strength of a self-assured adult, you now have the power to change the way you react to and interact with them. If you continue to interact with your family members with the psyche of a child, you inadvertently engineer the situation so that you are treated like a child. In contrast, you can be grounded in your reality as a self-sustained adult, break away from the toxic control cycle and start an adult-to-adult conversation. The chain of co-dependency cannot be sustained unless you are both engaged in it. For example, when you start asserting what you can and cannot give, they will have to renegotiate boundaries with you. Whilst your family members may or may not react in the way you have wished for, at least you know that you have done your part. Most of the time, however, when you interrupt the pattern of communication, change inevitably ripples through in the family system.

When the rubber hits the road

When we have a painful and traumatic experience, we often think we can 'get on with life' by splitting it off, never thinking about it, or erasing our memories entirely. But when you cut off healthy anger and the ability to assert yourself, you also cut off access to joy and aliveness. Your denial affects not just your relationships with people who have let you down, but also your present-day relationships with friends, partners and the wider community. It is only by allowing all of your genuine feelings – both anger and tenderness – to flow through, can you come alive, and enjoy authentic engagement with others.

Releasing the hurt from our past is not a linear, neat, once-and-for-all process. Real releasing that comes with long-lasting and substantial changes is, by its nature, cyclical and chaotic. At first, when you open the floodgates of your memory to allow in all of your past hurt, you may go through a period of intense oscillation between love and hate, resentment and gratitude, the need for attachment and distance. During this disconnecting time, you can anchor your heart in knowing that, although the unpleasant feelings are real and intense, they pose no true threat. Allowing them to go through your system is what ultimately liberates you. Do not be afraid if, in a moment of rage, you are unable to see love and peace on the horizon. Allow yourself to grieve, to be disappointed, to experience rage. It is safe to experience all shades of feelings; then, when your heart feels ready to return, it will find its way back to peace. At the end of this process, there may always be a part of you that remains scarred but, as the open wound heals, it remains just that – a scar. Even when triggered, it will no longer cause you to feel the same degree of emotional charge.

Forgiveness calls for you to grow out of black-and-white thinking and into understanding the complexity of relationships, which involves the paradoxes of love and anger, hurt and frustration. With the skill of integration you can love and be loved without approving, accepting or tolerating other people's bad behaviour. You can allow other people's hostility to pass you by without impulsively reacting to it. When cruelty comes your way, you can stand up for yourself without being aggressive. Even when you are disappointed, you may choose to hold both compassion for self and others in your heart. With newfound strength, you will allow yourself to grieve for what is not there so you can appreciate what is there. Your trauma does not have to take over your world, while at the same time, you do not need to reject your past to stay sane. In the end, you can embrace both your pain and joy as parts of your story.

At any given moment, you can drop the baggage of trauma from your family of origin. It is never too late to give yourself the freedom that you deserve.

Visualization exercises

Drop the baggage

Set aside at least half an hour for this visualization exercise. You may wish to have some paper and a pen ready, so you can doodle or write as you work through the process.

So often, even after we have left the nest of our family home, we carry physical, emotional and spiritual programming that has been installed in us. Consciously or unconsciously, we act out of mental imprints and behavioural patterns that have been passed down through generations. Now, close your eyes and imagine that you are carrying something that contains all of the dysfunctional values, beliefs, habits and world views you have inherited from your family. Visualize the object in a way that resonates with you. It may be a bag, a carton, a metal box, or any other shape or form. What colour is it? What material is it made of? In there, you may also find the trauma of sibling rivalries, your parents' criticism, shaming, projections, expectations or neediness. How heavy has your bag become? How big is it? Is it bigger than you are able to carry, or a manageable size? You may wish to draw or write down some of what you are visualizing.

Reflect on how you have been carrying this baggage for a very long time. You may have been burdened by it in the form of toxic shame, unfounded guilt, a permeating distrust of the world, low self-esteem or self-sabotage. Think about the opportunities, love and abundance it has blocked from you. Feel the weight this has created on your shoulders.

Imagine that sitting behind you are your parents and siblings. Envision their appearance, facial expressions and other qualities in your mind's eye. Now, when you are ready, turn around and, with a sense of empowerment, pass your baggage back to them. By doing so, you return whatever is in the baggage to where it rightly belongs. You may have to do this more than one time. Feel free to move your body to include the motion of pushing, dislodging and shaking.

You may say out loud something like 'Enough!', or 'I am ready to let this go!' You can also say something specific about your burden, for instance: 'Dear mother, I am returning the beliefs that "the world is not safe" to you' or 'Dear father, I am no longer carrying your shame for you'. Empty out everything that is in your baggage, until you feel light and free.

When it feels right to stop, take a few deep breaths. Notice how your body feels. You may feel a little shaky, but you may also find a sense of renewed spaciousness within you. Gently breathe while noticing any changes, and be reassured that healing will naturally take place.

Cut the cord

For the second exercise, think of a family member with whom you have an unhealthy or co-dependent relationship with. Imagine them standing in front of you with an energetic cord between you. Visualize what the cord looks like, see it extending from your belly to theirs, or from the palms of your hand to theirs. It might be a rope, a chain, a string or a beam of light. Let the materials, colour and texture of this cord represent the strength of your emotional ties and the quality of your attachment. You may wish to draw it out on a piece of paper.

Now, come up with an imaginary tool that can help you to cut the tie. It can be a pair of scissors, a sword, a knife, or something powerful. When you are ready, breathe in, set a loving intention for the greater good of both yourself and the other person, then, confidently cut the cord.

You are now free from a dysfunctional tie, so you can freely express your thoughts and feelings to them. Imagine telling your family member what you would have said if it was safe to do so. You can tell them what it has been like growing up in this family home, tell them about the hurt and trauma that has accumulated throughout the years, tell them about the needs and longings that were never met.

Register in your body how it feels to be completely honest.

Take a few moments to absorb any physiological changes after the exercise.

You can use this ritual to help yourself attain healthy individuation. Whether they are living or dead, emotionally separating from your parents is an essential step in your journey from healing to thriving. Cutting the cord does not mean you lose the person or the connection with them (although sometimes this may be necessary). What you cut is the unhealthy, co-dependent part of the relationship, and that will actually enhance and protect the healthy aspects of your bond.

6

Romantic and intimate relationships

Finding love while being you

Intense people are passionate lovers, but they face specific challenges due to their hyper-empathic tendencies, speed of operation, and high levels of intuition. In this chapter, we will discuss some of the obstacles you may face in intimate relationships (or the lack of them), and what you can do about them.

You feel bored and restless

Being intense, perhaps you operate at a pace that is mostly not shared by others. When your partner or potential partner falls behind you in their ability to grasp complexity and gather information, you cannot help but grow impatient. Since you are highly imaginative and energetic, you bring ideas and inspirations into the relationship that your partner does not have the capacity to reciprocate. You end up taking charge of most decisions and conversations, dominating the relationship without meaning to.

Your life is a constant intellectual and spiritual quest. You are enthusiastic about learning new things and are curious about the many mysteries in the world. Your other half may be content with the 'known', and not share your enthusiasm for various pursuits. Your search for novel experiences and mental challenges does not stop; if you expand your horizons and scope of consciousness at a much faster rate than your partner, you will have less and less in common. This creates a saddening situation where, although you care deeply for each other, the gap in your lifestyles, and level of personal development and spiritual depth can eventually become too much to bear. As this happens, you may feel under-stimulated and trapped in a two-person world.

You need significant time for solitude

You are imaginative and have a rich inner life. You have a wide range of interests, from art and music to politics. When you fall in love with a hobby, project or idea, your brain does not stop. When you are inspired, you work on overdrive; turning the lights out at night might not be what you want or need. You are making the best use of all the time you have, because inside you have always known you have the potential to achieve something great. If your partner doesn't function in the same way, however, they may think you are being excessive.

Creative and entrepreneurial endeavours require solitude to think about, and you need to exercise your imagination, but seclusion can come in short supply when you are in a committed relationship. You may focus on your inspired project for long periods and enjoy the challenges, but feel trapped in the movie theatre, or resent having to go to a dinner party. Compared with your own intellectual and spiritual ventures, you may find time spent with your partner increasingly unappealing. In turn, they may feel left out and make you feel guilty for needing more time to yourself.

You look for depth in a shallow world

Our increasingly shallow world is challenging for sensitive people, especially when it comes to the quest for love. The world is moving at a pace too fast for our souls, and the value of integrity is diminished. For example, research has found that people tend to represent how they want to be seen rather than who they actually are when dating online, and will lie for it.[1] As a truth seeker, this frustrates you. Getting to know someone requires patience and commitment, but these virtues are hard to come by. You need more time to get to know a person than the current social norm prescribes, and you may not be able to separate sex from an emotional and soulful connection. Your complexity alienates you from the crowd; being out of sync, it takes more time and effort for you to find people who are 'on your radar'.

Your partner does not understand your sensitivities

Many intense people have physical sensitivities – they get jumpy at loud noises, dislike too many sensory inputs, and need time to wind down after being in a crowd. When you are bombarded by stimuli, your body reacts with allergies, headaches, migraines, pain and fatigue. What excites your partners or potential partners can be aggravating for you – rollercoasters, loud music, constant background noise, humour that brings people down, overpowering perfume. Your needs are legitimate, though it may take clear and assertive communication to make things work in a partnership. If you were criticized by your other half for being 'too much', 'too dramatic', 'too difficult', and so on, it is crucial that you honour and stand up for yourself, and not buy into the idea that there is something wrong with you.

You pick up on every emotion and nuance

With your sensitivity comes intuition. You are highly perceptive and can pick up on many social nuances and small changes in human dynamics. Your gut instincts are especially astute when it comes to those who are close to you. When your partner is dishonest, you have a sense of it. When they are upset or angry, you know it even before they do. Due to your hyper-empathic tendencies, you 'absorb' whatever they feel, or even feel their feelings for them. Being the more emotionally aware one, you are almost always the one who initiates meaningful conversations or addresses issues in the relationship. Your sensitive perception creates two problems:

- Being an emotional sponge is exhausting for you. Without healthy emotional boundaries, you will burn out.
- Your partner feels intimidated or violated by you as you always see through them.

You prioritize others' needs before your own

Given your highly empathic nature, you may have always, in one way or another – either physically or emotionally, visibly or invisibly – played the role of a caretaker. If your parents were vulnerable or unavailable, it is most likely that you, as the most sensitive and intuitive child, stepped in as a 'mini-adult'. You might have been your siblings' and your parents' confidant, and even played the role of the therapist. Perhaps you had to grow up so fast, so soon, that you have been conditioned to prioritize others' needs before your own. It often feels like you are on autopilot, but you are so in tune with your partner's unvoiced needs and desires that you sometimes try to solve their problems even before they ask for help.

If you never had the chance to express your needs and have them met, it makes sense that you don't know how to seek help now. You tend not to share your distress or vulnerabilities with your partner, so even if they try to help you, they may feel like they are hitting a wall. This leaves both of you feeling alone in the relationship.

Suggestions for the intense ones

Reflect on the differences between a life partner and a soulmate

A longstanding cultural myth holds that we all need to have a 'special someone', but as an intense person, it can be almost impossible for you to find someone who can meet you in all dimensions – physically, emotionally, spiritually, intellectually. Perhaps the person you are sexually attracted to is emotionally distant, or those you feel the most connected to fail to keep up with intellectual debates. A useful strategy here may be to reflect on the difference between a 'life partner' and a 'soulmate', and to question if they need to be the same person.

A life partner is a trustworthy companion. They are your co-pilot when handling life-tasks such as homemaking and parenting. They are your best friend and support system. You may not or no longer have an electrifying spiritual connection with them, but they make you feel calm and loved.

A soulmate is someone who can meet the depth of your soul. This person follows your fast train of thoughts, joins you in your imagination, gets excited about your vision, and sees what you intuitively see. They get your humour, challenge you to think and learn, and you are never 'too much' for them. When you are with them, you feel exhilarated, instantly understood, and communication is effortless.

In psychology, the theory of love differentiates between compassionate love and passionate love. Compassionate love involves feelings of mutual respect and trust, while passionate love involves intense feelings and 'a state of intense longing for union'.[2] The former is what we have with a life partner, whilst the latter is what we feel when we are infatuated with a soulmate.

Some intense people are lucky enough to have found a soulmate to be their life partner. But others spend their lives searching for the person who is the 'perfect match' in all aspects, only to be disappointed every time.

If you can separate the role of a life partner and that of a soulmate, you can then reflect on your priorities and design your life accordingly. You may be content with having a life partner who is not a soulmate and seek intellectual stimulation, emotional connection and spiritual union elsewhere. After all, your soulmate can be a friend, teacher, they can even be a family member. Alternatively, you can choose to make it your mission to search for your one soulmate and refuse to compromise. There is no right or wrong; it is a matter of honouring your needs. However, being able to be clear about what you want and choosing your course will save you from resentments, internal conflict and misdirected efforts.

Avoid the blame game – it is not because you are 'too intense'!

We all have our default defence mechanisms – or coping strategies – and yours may clash with your partner's. When you are in a relationship, you may find that you are stuck in a repetitive conflict loop, where the same pattern repeats itself. A common pattern among couples is the pursuer–withdrawer dynamic, where one of you plays the role of the pursuer and the other the withdrawer. If you are a pursuer, you want to maintain contact with others even in times of conflict. Rather than letting things lie or leaving them to cool off, you would rather keep a heated conversation going. When you feel unsure, you reach out for reassurance and support. If your partner blocks you off, you try even harder to get through; you may raise your voice, criticize your partner, or pressure them for a response. To you, just because someone is not directly confrontational does not mean they are not provocative. Passivity can be aggravating, and giving the 'silent treatment' can be more hurtful than words. As the withdrawer, they will view your attempts to engage as pushy, or even attacking.

Many intense people are pursuers but, dependent on your early life experience and attachment style, you may also play the role of a withdrawer in a relationship. As a withdrawer, you look for ways to exit conflicts. You need to shut down to avoid being overwhelmed, precisely because you feel emotions so intensely. Instead of working things through with your partner, you would rather work things through in your own space first. You may avoid eye contact, turn away, walk away or remain silent. You try to keep peace by distancing yourself. When your partner is raging, you may feel it is unsafe to proceed with saying or doing anything, and only when they calm down do you feel it is safe enough to re-engage.

When a couple argues, each side is tempted is to drive all blame onto the other, or resort to attacking each other personally. By seeing the wider picture, however, you can see that the process is reciprocal and not one-sided; you both participate in, and sustain, the pattern. For example, if your partner did not withdraw, you would not have to pursue. Conversely, if you did not raise your voice, they may feel more ready to open up. You feel unheard, unloved and dismissed, and may seek reassurance even more energetically. At the same time, your partner feels smothered, pressured or attacked and may close down even more. You are locked in a pattern whereby each person's coping strategies are exacerbated.

When you get caught in a back-and-forth that feels all too familiar, take a step back. Try not to fall into the trap of carrying all the blame, especially when your partner attacks you for being 'too sensitive' or 'too much'. At the same time, recognize your part in the dance, and the shadow traits that you may not be seeing in yourself. As much as possible, shift your focus from the surface-layer conflicts to the longings and vulnerabilities that lie underneath. Embedded within both coping strategies are emotional needs that yearn to be attended to. Underlying the need to pursue are the fear of abandonment and emotional loneliness. Beneath the need to withdraw may be unprocessed and dissociated trauma around anger and aggression, feelings of helplessness, and a sense of failure as a partner. Shifting your focus towards the emotional wounds and needs of both yourself and your partner allows you to remember your shared humanity, so you can shift away from blame and towards empathy and compassion.

Communication mismatch

Communication mismatch is another common issue faced by intense people in relationships, especially when each partner has a different way of functioning in the world.

One of the most common complaints among couples is that one person interrupts and does not let the other person finish speaking.[3] It turns out that people differ in their expectations of how long one person can speak for during a conversation, and how much detail they can tolerate. Some of these differences can be explained by personality systems such as the Myers–Briggs Type Indicator (MBTI). In MBTI, the preference towards either Sensing or Intuition function describes how a person processes information. Sensors focus on what is present and factual. They tend to be concrete, literal thinkers who value practicalities. In contrast, Intuitive people process information through seeing patterns, using metaphors and relying on impressions. They are imaginative and value inspirations more than the literal meaning of things.

The difference between the Intuitive Function and the Sensing Function determines each person's primary focus in a conversation. Intuitives are interested in the bigger picture, whereas Sensors tend to focus on observable details. The majority of the population are Sensors, but intense people tend to be Intuitives. The preferences are not set in stone, you can also fall between the two functions. If Intuition is your predominant function, you may find that in a conversation your Sensor partner constantly interrupts you to try and gather or correct information. For them, the facts must be correct before the story continues. Whereas for you, these details are not as important as the flow of the story and the bigger idea.[4]

As an Intuitive, you love contemplating possibilities and new ideas. When you are stimulated, you jump from one point to another, painting the 'big picture' and skipping over the details. You may also have a divergent thinking style, so your mind works by drawing wild associations between ideas that freely follow the lead of your imagination. On the receiving end, your Sensor partner may have difficulty keeping up with your abstract ideas and trains of thought. They prefer language that is precise, specific, and lined up from point A to point B. Your tendency to 'jump around' without landing anywhere is unsettling. As the speaker, you are annoyed when they seem to impulsively respond to specifics that you don't think are relevant, or have an almost obsessive need to correct anything that doesn't sound quite right, thereby disrupting your flow. To you, they miss the forest for the trees. On the other hand, as a listener you find it difficult to listen to a lot of details, and are more concerned with understanding the ideas and logic behind it. Rather than staying present and concentrating on what they are saying, your mind is busy generating in-depth insights.

Practically, there may be simple solutions to your challenges. Couple's therapist Ellen Wachtel suggests setting up ahead of time how long each party ought to listen before interjecting.[5] Rather than letting the other person get impatient and interrupt, the speaker can, from time to time, acknowledge that their partner has been listening for a long time, and invite their input. It is important that the listener feels that they are being talked to, rather than talked at.

Communication mismatch becomes a complicated issue when it brings back past trauma or involves deeper dynamic issues. On their own, however, these differences could be reconciled, or even harnessed, to promote growth and intimacy. Always try to bear in mind that you are born with different ways of perceiving and different ways of being in the world. Each style has its advantages and neither is superior. Sometimes, your partner's disinterest in the theoretical and the abstract is a strength. Perhaps their fine eye for detail may be exactly what you need to bring your abstract big vision into fruition. Their down-to-earth quality helps you reality-check when your imagination runs wild. You do not need your partner to be your intellectual equal. They are not the source of your insights – you are. If you can let them know that their mere presence is enough, they can also be relieved from the pressure of having to keep up with you. And if they do not feel as much pressure to be useful to you, they may not feel the need to interject so often.

There is beauty in personality clashes. While they can be challenging on a day-to-day level, they can also be your relationship's biggest asset.

Manage your relationship expectations

You can change and control many things in life, but another person's temperament is not one of them.

In a healthy relationship, each party must learn to see and receive the other person's unique 'love language', without insisting that their own needs are met in exactly the ways they want them to be met. People have different modes, frequencies and strengths when it comes to their expression of love. For example, your loved one may offer a consistent and calming presence, but is lacking when it comes to actual solutions or physical efforts. They may show love via productive actions but remain emotionally avoidant. They may be someone who isn't able to shower you with beautiful words, but you know you can count on them in moments of crisis. For others, you may never see roses by your pillow, but the house chores are always taken care of.

If you can take a step back from your fixed frame of reference of 'how things should be', you open the door to a full range of love expression that you were missing before. Even at times when you feel let down, try and adopt a compassionate perspective, and contemplate your partners' prohibitions, insecurities and vulnerabilities. Ask yourself: what trauma might be constraining their expression of love? If they cannot express themselves in words, what are their actions saying? Seeing their limitations lucidly may change your perspective: what if what you see as rejection is really love expressed clumsily? What if the abandonment you feel is actually how they feel, but that feeling is projected outward? Could it be that, more than you, they too are frustrated with their limitations?

No one person, not even a soulmate, can meet your needs in all dimensions. Relationships are never perfect, and they are not meant to be. Embedded in every disappointment, irritation and conflict are lessons designed to grow and stretch you. They invite your idealist mind to collaborate with reality and challenge your childlike expectations that always want things to go your way. They stop you from turning your romantic partner into a surrogate parent and challenge you to find home within yourself.

One of the biggest milestones in maturing as a person is learning to accept and gain nourishment from reality as it is, rather than the way you want it. This does not mean passivity or inaction, but wise efforts. By discerning what is within your power to change and what is not, you can invest your hope and energy accordingly. 'Grieve what is absent and harness gratitude for what is present' is a life lesson that will enrich not just your relationships but your life as a whole. Far from being a hindrance, an imperfect relationship is a place where you train to become a resilient adult who can hold paradoxes and tensions and enjoy the world as it is – even with all its imperfections.

Be mindful of the temptation to close up

Having been hurt and betrayed before, either in childhood or in previous relationships, you might have built a wall or a shield around yourself. This is not a conscious action but an automatic protective mechanism. Like the barrier in an electric circuit, your system shuts down when the pain gets too much. You now have a thought pattern that says, 'I don't need anyone', 'People are not dependable', 'It is risky to trust someone', 'People can hurt me, and I may not survive it this time'. Your shield manifests in different ways, such as emotional detachment, feeling empty, social avoidance, a facade of being aloof and arrogant, cynicism and the tendency to over-intellectualize everything. You may numb your heart via keeping busy, drugs and alcohol, addictions of all kinds, or presenting a sociable persona while keeping exchanges with others superficial. You curb your passion and guard your feelings. You stop yourself from falling in love and are sure not to be vulnerable with people. Your mask might have allowed you to feel safe and more in control but it leaves you in an arid place. Freezing your capacity to love is a childlike way of defending against life and is not sustainable.

Breaking out of your numbness requires a gradual process of compassion and self-love. Rather than seeing it as your enemy, be kind and tender towards your need to close up. Becoming aware of it is the first step, and then you can investigate the root of it. You were once traumatized, but you are now much stronger than you once were. Although you cannot prevent disappointments in life, you will be able to get past them. Taking one small step at a time, you will be able to open your heart again to intimacy. Even relationships come with their risks and perils, it is a worthwhile endeavour.

(We will address this issue in more depth later in this chapter, in 'The flight from intimacy'.)

Show up as you

Having been out of sync with others all your life, and having internalized all the 'too' criticisms ('too serious', 'too intense', 'too complex', 'too emotional', etc.), you may have a hard time loving yourself. If your upbringing was not supportive of your sensitivity, you would not know how to embrace it. As you are used to being everyone's emotional caretaker, you have a hard time being the champion of your right to be unconditionally loved. Loving yourself starts from knowing yourself. You must make time to clarify what matters to you – your values, beliefs and priorities, and know that you deserve to go after what you need.

It is paramount that you allow yourself the right to expression. In the past, stepping into the spotlight might have attracted envy and attack from others, and that has taught you to trade authenticity for safety. You may have spent your life trying to hide, to conform, and to be silent. This protective strategy has expired. Right now, the only way you can find people who appreciate you with your intensity is when you show up with it.

The goal of your life is not to perfect yourself, but to perfect your love for yourself. Regardless of whether or not you find romance in the world, you can learn to embrace yourself in totality, including both your positive and your negative traits, the charming and annoying things about you. It is not what you look like, how much you do, and who you attract that make you deserve love. You are worthy and deserving as you are a creation of nature. Like every tree and flower have their distinct shape and size, it is your birthright to shine as you are. Please don't deprive the world of your light – someone like you is looking for you, and they can only find you if you show up as who you are.

Stop trying to control the outcome, seize every day as they come

As an intense and competent person, you are used to being in the driver's seat. In romance, however, the law of effort and results does not apply. You have little control over who you will meet and when, how it happens, and what happens next.

When it comes to something as intangible as love and relationships, you can practise what the Buddhists call the 'beginner's mind', or the 'don't know mind'. When you look back in life, you know that you never know what will happen – what you had rejected might turn out to be a portal to fortune, and what you had been charmed by could turn out to be the beginning of an inferno. We so often want what we don't need and neglect the gifts that are right under our noses. Therefore, let go of your attachment to outcomes. You can have desires, you can set intentions; you can work towards finding the love you want and keeping the love you already have, but try to avoid falling into the illusion of control. You can simultaneously hold your power to take action and the willingness to release fixation over a particular outcome; it is always a balancing act.

Life is not a waiting room. If you wait for the perfect romance to happen before you begin living your life, you can be waiting forever.

> Even if you are not content with what you have in the present moment, remind yourself that you will have this moment only once, and one day you will miss today.

Summon gratitude for what you have, rather than focusing on what is lacking. Each moment in life, including the waiting, the loneliness, the separation, the longing and the sorrow, are all essential pieces of the tapestry that makes up your life. Acceptance of the present moment does not mean surrendering to non-action. It means you bring loving awareness to each moment of your life, so that at the end of it, you know you have lived it fully, regardless of what has happened.

Your invitation to love

If I were to give you only one piece of advice, it would be to never sacrifice your vitality and passion for a false sense of safety or security. You might have dreamed and fallen, you might have despaired and lost all hope, but it is through the cracks that the light comes through. Regardless of the severity of your hurt, it is only temporary. By deadening your soul, however, you sell time you will never get back to the devil. Life is a dance between dark and light, pleasure and pain, trust and betrayal. Love is like that, too. Small risks will follow you wherever you go, but you also have the infinite strength to withstand all of the storms thrown at you. Love and fall; get back up and love again. On the last day of your life, you will look back and realize that it is the peaks and valleys that make this journey worthwhile.

Journaling exercise: 'when i am in love...'

Using a visual journal, fill in the blanks and write statements/ poetry using the following prompts.

Try not to overthink, or worry about the implications of your statements.

Allow the playful, spontaneous side of you to take hold. No matter what emerges, this can be valuable information that informs your next step in life.

When I am in love, I am _____.

To me, a life partner is _____.

To me, a soulmate is ____.

____ makes me excited.

____ makes me feel safe.

To me, a fulfilling relationship means ____.

In my wildest fantasy, I ____.

It is important that I feel ____.

I would never say it, but I want others to know that I am ____.

In a relationship, I often act as if ____.

My biggest worry in a relationship is that ____.

I regret ____.

I feel the most loved when ____.

I am the most fulfilled in life when ____.

I feel bored and under-stimulated when ____.

I close up when ____.

I wish I could release ____.

I am worried that I ____.

I love myself the most when ____.

From my partner/partners, I want ____.

From my partner/partners, I need ____.

Review the sentences you have completed. What about them is powerful, surprising or revealing?

What do your statements say about your current values, needs and desires?

What can you do to move towards a more fulfilling romantic life?

The fear of abandonment

Some degree of anxiety is a normal part of human relationships. Being attracted to and attached to someone makes us feel vulnerable, and intimate relationships are often where old fears from our unhealed past emerge. We can broadly categorize our relationship fears into two camps:

- The fear of being abandoned/rejected
- The fear of being engulfed/smothered/losing oneself.

In this chapter, we focus on the fear of abandonment. Having a fear of being left behind by someone you love and depend on is not a pathology in itself; it is a primal fear that is hardwired into our survival mechanism. It only becomes dysfunctional if you are subsumed by your fears or let them drive all your behaviours. When you have severe fear of abandonment, you may have unrealistic demands, projections and expectations. To help you find the way out of this sabotaging pattern, we will explore the concept of object constancy, early experiences that might have created this fear, and how you can stop bringing the past into the present.

Do you struggle with the fear of abandonment?

Here are some signs that indicate you may struggle with an excessive fear of abandonment:

- Even in a long-term relationship, you are constantly in doubt. Will my loved one be there when I need them? Do I matter? Will I be rejected if I express my true feelings?
- You feel hollow when people you are attached to are not by your side.

- You live with an inexplicable anxiety that someone important to you will be hurt, killed, or will suddenly disappear.
- You are hypervigilant, always watching out for signs that your partner may be pulling away.
- When others are 'out of sight', you do not believe they still have you on their mind.
- You cope with loneliness through addictive behaviours like drinking or gambling, compulsive rituals, overworking, or by becoming emotionally numb.
- You feel triggered by even the most subtle signs of disapproval or criticisms. When others don't explicitly express praise or affection, you worry about their opinions of you.
- You compare yourself to others and believe you are less desirable or lovable. You seek constant validation and reassurance from others, yet when they give you compliments, you struggle to take them in.
- You have a tendency, especially at the beginning of a relationship, to idealize people and become obsessed with them.
- Your feelings towards others swing between extremes. One day, they are the love of your life, and the next day you decide to withdraw your trust completely. Sometimes dependence feels like the only option; at other times, you do not want to invest any hope.
- You long for affection, but when it is given you assume it will soon disappear, and cannot wholeheartedly enjoy the intimacy.
- You go for romance that will not be reciprocated because deep down you do not believe you can have the love you desire.

- You attach easily and ignore 'red flags' when committing to someone. You may also overstay in unhealthy relationships. When the other person leaves, you blame yourself for not being good enough.
- You hold grievances for longer than you would like to and ruminate over events in which you feel you have been wronged.
- When there is a conflict, you may have the bad habit of storming off, on the assumption that you can return whenever you are ready. You underestimate the strain this puts on the relationship until your partner threatens to leave.
- You put a lot of energy into caring for others and feel resentful later when your efforts are not reciprocated. You are often hurt by other people's thoughtlessness.
- Your feelings towards your loved ones are mixed; you seek closeness but get angry about their unavailability, so you oscillate between being pushy and being helpless.
- You become so distracted by relationship stress that you have a hard time focusing at work or on your vocation.

What causes you to have so much fear?

There can be many causes for excessive fear of abandonment, from a bad relationship experience to post-traumatic stress. In attachment theory, fear of abandonment is closely related to an attachment style known as 'anxious ambivalent'. You may develop this pattern when your early caregivers are inconsistent, unstable or invasive. It can also happen if an early formative experience – such as a previous marriage – has left scars in you in a similar way.

If love was inconsistent

Fear of abandonment can be a result of having received love in a highly inconsistent way. Perhaps as a child, your caregivers were nice one day and cruel the next, warm one day and cold another. Your parents may not have had the capacity to tolerate closeness; they were afraid of the tender and vulnerable feelings that emerge in authentic exchanges, so whenever they felt their guard slipping, they immediately shut down. You may have found that, just as you started to share a warm and intimate moment with them, they abruptly made a harsh comment, put you down or did something to push you away. You were then left feeling shock and disappointment, even beating yourself up for having trusted in the first place. As you faced the constant threat of abandonment, you never got to internalize a sense of security. Your hunger for love was fed occasionally and partially, but never fully. You could not relax with this push–pull behaviour, and were always on the look-out for the next sudden withdrawal of affection or anger blow-out.

Perhaps your parents were not entirely rejecting. Worse, they were sometimes rejecting and sometimes loving. This fluctuation kept the possibility open for you to get what you needed, and made it hard for you to give up hope. In your attempt to win their love, you may have become the 'good child', pleasing them however you could; or you protested with tantrums and anger. Since your needy behaviour occasionally got you what you needed, you were tempted to keep trying. Eventually, this pattern of oscillating between rage and clinginess became an addictive cycle. Even if you no longer behave in the same way around your parents, when an intimate partner enters your life these attachment behaviours repeat themselves.

If you have highly anxious parents

Due to their own lack of maturity and capacity, highly anxious parents might let their own shortcomings override their children's need for autonomy and growth. By smothering you with overprotection, they may have undermined your confidence by limiting your opportunities to explore the world, to make your own mistakes and to learn from experience. In this way, you may have been held back from achieving your developmental goals, forming healthy relationships and gaining a sense of self-agency. Having absorbed their separation anxieties, you now experience your own need for autonomy as a betrayal and feel guilty about it. In other words, you have been conditioned to fear separation and to believe you cannot stand on your own two feet. Unlike blatantly abusive parents, anxious parents do not mean to frighten their children, but they were scared children themselves once. Through their fretfulness and their tendency to catastrophize, they indoctrinate their children with the message that 'the world is a dangerous place' and 'people can't be trusted'. Since they are highly controlling in their attempts to protect their family, their fears about the world are passed down trans-generationally; their separation anxiety becomes their children's fear of abandonment, who even as grown-ups struggle to let go of what they have inherited.

Understanding object constancy

To understand the psychology behind excessive abandonment fears, let's examine a concept in psychology called 'object constancy' – the ability to feel that an emotional bond remains intact even when there is a conflict, disagreement or distance.

Object constancy is related to a cognitive ability called 'object permanence'. Object permanence is the understanding that objects continue to exist even when they are hidden, or cannot be seen, heard or touched. If you have ever played peek-aboo with babies, you see how when you hide your face from them, they will think you have ceased to exist. When you put a toy under a blanket, they will start to search for it. Because they have not yet developed object permanence, they can only hold in their mind what they can definitely see.

While object permanence concerns physical objects, object constancy is about the ability to hold others in your mind, and to believe that you are being held in mind by others, even when there are temporary distances, absences or conflicts. If your childhood experience was stable and nourishing, you would have managed to internalize a sense of safety inside yourself, and you do not need others to always be by your side to know that you are loved. In contrast, if the parenting you received was chaotic, inconsistent or invasive, you were deprived of the opportunity to internalize inner resources for self-soothing, self-containment and self-encouragement. You end up with a constant need for an external object to fill an internal void.

Without object constancy, you relate to others as 'parts', rather than as a 'whole'. Like a child who cannot comprehend the mother as a complete person – who sometimes rewards and sometimes frustrates, you struggle to hold the paradox that both yourself and others have both good and bad aspects. You may experience relationships as unreliable, making you vulnerable, and dependent on your mood of the moment.

As grown-ups, we need object constancy to enjoy and feel satisfaction in relationships. With object constancy, even when a loved one is not by your side, telling you where they are or reassuring you, you still feel connected to them because you trust that you have a place in their heart. Without object constancy, temporary absence feels like a disappearance or abandonment. Your fear of abandonment is triggered when your loved one is not around, picking up the phone, or replying to your texts. When they need some space away, you feel desolate. When you get into a fight, you struggle to bounce back from the conflict and to believe things are okay again. Since you are questioning the coming and going of another person, and doubting their love, you live in constant fear.

Healing the past in the present

We often, albeit unconsciously, look to our current relationships to fulfil our deepest unfulfilled needs and longings, to plug the gaps in our psyches, and to heal where we have been wounded. In psychoanalysis, this is called 'transference'. We want from our intimate others what we were deprived of in our early lives, often by our family of origin. We repeat the same story but are secretly hoping for a different outcome.

When triggered, perhaps your fear of abandonment evokes raw and extreme reactions. You may scream, shout, become clingy, demanding and possessive. After you have acted out, shame and self-blame follow, further derailing your relationship and your sense of self. In transference, you face a painful double-bind: you want to push people away in case they hurt you again, but you also want them close to fulfil your deep longings. This might have been the same conundrum you felt as a child, being at the mercy of unreliable caregivers. To those around you, your reactions to distance seem disproportionate. However, it is not your fault that you act that way. You are having an emotional flashback to the survival fears you had in childhood. You are making a desperate attempt to, in symbolic form, win the love of the parents who are supposed to be there. If you think of yourself as acting from a place of repressed or dissociated trauma – and consider what it is like for a two-year-old to be left alone – the intense fear, anger and despair all makes sense. Seeing this, you may begin to approach yourself with self-compassion, rather than further denigration.

If you are haunted by abandonment fears, it is likely that you have been trapped in frozen grief without realizing it. What has been lost here is the archetypal father and mother, an innocent childhood, a sense of security, a feeling of home, and the belief that you are special to someone. You are seeking the image of an ideal parent in your partner because you are stuck in shock and disbelief about what you have missed. All children have a developmental need to have someone they see as 'all-power-ful, omniscient and perfect'[6]; the Superman appeals universally because it speaks to our fundamental longing. Being exposed to too many of your parents' limitations too early and too soon was traumatizing because it went against your innate needs. You were not an orphan from the outset. Instead, you had a tantaliz-ing taste of love and safety, yet it was taken away from you. That is why you have devoted your life to looking for the symbolic ideal. In the trench of your search for a parental replacement, you see yourself as small and dependent and project your power outward. Since your partner represents your heroic role model, when you have a glimpse of their limitations, you become dis-proportionately disappointed and frustrated. Underlying your insatiable demand is a quest for love. However, this sets an impos-sible task. After all, the weight of your unmourned hopes and lost childhood are too heavy to be carried by an adult relation-ship. To move forward, you must mourn the childhood that you did not have, and relate to your partner as an adult. As grown-ups, true intimacy requires two autonomous people who enjoy times of closeness as well as time apart. Each party should have a mind of his or her own, and that is to be celebrated. Your needs, wishes and personalities are not tangled up with theirs. Unlike the symbiosis with your parents, you must learn where you end, and others begin.

Cultivating object constancy means coming to terms with the complexity of reality – you must learn to see that people can love you and sometimes disappoint you, and that someone you love also has their own life and may sometimes need distance. If you are able to hold both the faults and the virtues in yourself and others, you will not have to resort to the primitive defence of 'splitting' or black-or-white thinking. You do not have to constantly test their love, or devalue your partner because they have disappointed you at one point. With practice, you learn that people can be limited and good enough at the same time, that they may need their distance, even though they hold you dearly in their heart. Even when there are occasional conflicts, the emotional foundation underneath the surface ripples can remain solid. Eventually, you will also grow to be compassionate with yourself, and see that just because you are not perfect all the time does not mean you are 'bad', or unworthy of love.

Achieving object constancy is a developmental milestone because it gives you the ability to tolerate ambiguity and uncertainty. With this skill, you begin to grapple with the fact that human relationships experience ebb and flow. Just like we need to breathe in to breathe out, contract to expand, a healthy relationship requires a dynamic flow between closeness and distance, ups and downs, disappointment and fulfilment. Your relationship is similar to a dance, or to music – there is no closeness without distance, no music without pauses. If you fixate only on the times you are together and ignore the empty spaces, you stifle the pulsation, and squander the relationship.

Your abandonment fear is overpowering because your survival once depended on it, but your fear no longer reflects your current reality. As an adult, you know that people can break promises, withhold their love, and change the way they act; but you also know that these things can no longer traumatize you. Not only can you survive disappointment and loneliness, but you can also say no to abusive relationships and walk away. You can no longer be 'abandoned' – if a relationship comes to an end, it is the natural consequence of a mismatch in two people's values, needs, and life paths. By separating the past from the present, you can meet your partners as they are, not under the filters of projections and false expectations. You realize they do not need to be perfect, as they do not reflect on you, represent you, or limit you. You can hold their good and bad together in your heart without flipping into black-or-white thinking. By cultivating emotional resilience and the ability to self-soothe, you do not count on others to create a safe haven for you, you can do it for yourself.

Sometimes, when locked in a bubble of fear, we forget that as a species, we are wired to love, to connect, and to be in love. We come into this world with built-in faculties to adapt to changes, to bounce back from heartbreaks, and to give and receive love. It is not that you don't have feelings or will never feel hurt, but you are strong enough to weather the storms, and also reap the joy of being in love. Even though the journey is precarious, it is a worthwhile and essential one.

Practical strategy: create a self-companion box

The practical exercise for this chapter is to make a self-companion box. This is a box you make purely for yourself; it contains resources you can access during the times when you feel lonely, sad, or plagued by fears of abandonment.

There is no right or wrong way to make a self-companion box. It can be of any size or shape and be made with any materials. You may use a cardboard box, a biscuit tin or a wooden carton. This is wholly made for yourself and not for the sake of showing anyone. You can start small and gradually add to it. There is no pressure for perfection.

The box will be used as a tool to steady yourself when, occasionally, you slip into an emotional downward spiral, or find yourself regressing to black-or-white thinking. Just as you notice the beginning of an emotional storm, you can use the contents of this box to self-soothe, or interrupt a negative chain of thought.

Here is a list of things you may want to include in your self-companion box:

- A picture of someone you feel warmly towards: Choose a person with whom you have a warm and uncomplicated relationship. This may also be a pet, a deceased relative, or an old friend. When you see this picture, it evokes feelings of tenderness and compassion in you, and reminds you of what it feels to love and be loved.
- Relationship cue cards: Collaborate with your partner; ask him or her to write down words of reassurance on a piece of paper. You can read this when there is conflict or distance, to remind yourself that, despite the temporary ripples, your partner's love for you remains undisturbed.
- Soothing object: This can be anything that is grounding and calming for you. When extreme emotions are triggered, you can use a range of sensory objects to focus your mind or to self-soothe. You can include something that smells good, feels good or even tastes good. For example, a piece of soft cloth, a cooling piece of crystal, a pebble, a bottle of essential oil, a sweet.
- Diffusion activities: Make a list of self-soothing or enjoyable activities that you can do to distract yourself from a negative mental loop. You can include small tools such as art materials or adult colouring books to work with.
- A postcard from your future self: Write a letter to the part of you that is experiencing abandonment fears. You

can remind yourself that, regardless of how you feel, these emotions will pass, and that you are worthy of love.

- A list of your strengths and lovable qualities: You can ask your friends and family to help you make this list. In times of relationship crisis, when you are experiencing strong emotions around attachment and abandonment, being able to read about the positive aspects of yourself from the perspective of others can be reassuring. Alongside this, you may want to add letters or keepsakes from your loved ones.

- Motivational quotes or images: Collect physical or digital images that inspire you to think bigger and to take a wider perspective. You can collect quotes from films, books, and poems, and find images you like from Pinterest and Instagram. You may also create some positive mantras or statements that you can read out loud to yourself.

- A playlist of music that calms or uplifts your spirit: You can download certain guided meditations or music to your phone.

Put your box where it can be easily seen and accessed. You can also have a 'pocket version' of these resources that you carry with you.

Every time you use the self-companion box when you feel wobbly, you are summoning your inner resources to restore your physiological and emotional balance. With repeated practice, a neural pathway of self-resourcing will be built in your brain, deepening the fabric of resilience. This acts as an inner anchor that helps you weather the inevitable ebb and flow in relationships. Slowly but surely, your ability to self-soothe will replace the old memories of being abandoned or trapped in a push-pull dynamic with your original caregivers. Instead of despair and dependency, inner calm and self-compassion will become your new defaults.

The flight from intimacy

In the last chapter, we discussed the fear of abandonment. In this chapter, we will examine something that, at first glance, appears to be on the other end of the spectrum: the fear of intimacy and engulfment.

The flight from intimacy is a pattern that governs how you relate to the world. It is brought about by a hyper-alert defence system that is primed to detect intrusion. Your psyche feels threatened when people come close to you, initiate contact with you, express desires for you, or want commitment from you. As you deny the need for closeness and become cut off from your emotions, you may operate on auto-pilot, and end up feeling empty and numb.

The flight from intimacy is not the opposite of the fear of abandonment, sometimes it is a way of coping with it. Just as anorexia can be a defence against bulimia, you suppress your longings for closeness as a result of an emotionally deprived childhood. Since you have had enough of painful disappointment, you have unconsciously decided that it would be easier if you were to never trust or depend on anyone.

Why you have given up

As children, we need our early caregivers to validate our sense of worthiness through a process called 'mirroring'. In healthy relating, your parents acknowledge how you feel, reflect things back to you and help you regulate distress. When you smile, they smile back at you. When you are anxious, they empathize with you while demonstrating a calming presence. It is through this back-and-forth process that you learn to manage your emotions and gain a sense of self-worth. Your parents can show you that you are unique, wanted and welcome by explicitly praising you and acknowledging your worth, but often it is the more subtle clues – gestures, expression, or a tone of voice – that matter more.

Due to their immaturity, mental illness, undiagnosed neuro-atypical traits (such as autistic spectrum, Asperger's or ADHD), extreme work or health demands, your parents might not have been emotionally responsive to you. Instead of providing the necessary mirroring, they are cold, critical, or dismissive. They were put off when you sought attention and avoided touching or playing with you. Or, they were physically present but emotion-ally blank. They might have reacted contemptuously to your call for connection, condemned you for being 'too much' or allowed your siblings to mock you for being sensitive. Some parents are afraid of conflicts or any intense emotions. When you cry or get angry, they panic, and in turn punish you for what they feel. When you have emotionally blank and dismissive parents, the messages you have learned about the world says that people are not trustworthy, you cannot connect to them, and that you are unworthy of love.[7]

While emotional neglect or abuse is harmful to all chil-dren, it is especially crippling for the intense and sensitive ones. Given their heightened perceptive abilities, they readily pick up on any contempt or dismissal. Shame is then imprinted on the developing brain as an implicit memory.[8] Although inter-nalized shame lies below consciousness, it dominates life and relationships in unthinkable ways.

Current evidence suggests that emotional neglect can com-promise the development of certain brain areas. Neuro-biolog-ically, the lack of positive attunement from caregivers affects the hippocampal volume, a brain structure responsible for emotional regulation.[9] Neglect also blunts the development of the ventral striatum, a critical component of your motivational system.[10] As a result of a neglected upbringing, a sensitive child can easily feel depressed and helpless, and will certainly have a higher risk of developing depression.[11] They are also more likely than others to dissociate and detach from their body.

The trauma of neglect and contempt lies not in what happened but in what did not happen. Since it is difficult to put invisible suffering into words, instead of expressing and processing it, as a highly sensitive person you find ways to live with it. To cope with the buried pain of being unseen and unheard you might employ a myriad of psychological and behavioural strategies, all of which are designed around the avoidance of intimacy. These strategies may be conscious and unconscious, functional or maladaptive. Counter-dependency, social isolation, emotional and intimacy anorexia are ways you might have adopted in order to navigate the social landscape, while intellectualizing, emotional detachment and excessive daydreaming are ways you might try to organize your inner world. We will take a deeper look at each of them.

Strategies you have adopted to avoid intimacy

Counter-dependency

You probably have heard of the phrase 'co-dependency', which refers to a dysfunctional lack of separation between two people and their emotional worlds. What is less known and spoken about is 'counter-dependency', a form of extreme self-reliance. If co-dependency is not trusting that you could survive without another person, counter-dependency is not being able to trust other people – to take care of you, to be depended upon for big and small practical tasks, or to lean on for comfort or consolation. Counter-dependency is likely linked to the avoidant attachment style. In a series of empirical research projects, it was shown that even in stressful or threatening situations such as military training and being close to death, avoidantly attached people tend not to seek support, but would instead distance themselves from people, including significant others.[12]

Perhaps as a child you tried to seek comfort from those who were supposed to take care of you, but were repeatedly disappointed. You might have cried and protested, but were only ever met with coldness, hostility, or abandonment. Your experience has taught you that revealing vulnerabilities is pointless or even risky, so in the end you gave up wanting anything from anyone at all. As a grown-up, you make sure you can absolutely stand on your own two feet. You believe seeking help is a form of weakness, and strong emotions should be avoided at all cost.

Apart from having volatile or vulnerable parents, your experience among peer groups may have played a part in developing counter-dependency. Since you were gifted and mature beyond your years, you were constantly under-stimulated by those around you. Your peers either struggled to keep up with you, or they wanted something from you. There was no one you could truly depend on or to look up to. You might also have been scapegoated or become the target of others' envious attacks. Since your experience with other people has been unfulfilling, draining or threatening, you resort to seeking kinship not from people, but from avenues such as solitude, spirituality, books and music. You may compulsively accumulate knowledge, power, wealth and social status. These pursuits give you a sense of safety and an illusion of control. A part of you believes that by hoarding enough resources, you will never have to ask anyone for anything.

Counter-dependency is not sustainable in the long run. The reality is that we live in an interdependent world, and complete control or autonomy is an illusion. Being emotionally self-contained is healthy, but that is different from a defensive denial of our need to belong.

In mature independence, we are self-sufficient but do not deny our longing for relationships and the inevitable ties we have with the rest of humanity.

Keeping people at arm's length

Through counter-dependency, you limit your dependency on others. But sometimes it is not enough to make sure that you do not depend on anyone – you also feel the need to avoid any potential dependency on you. To do so, you limit not only romantic attachments, but all forms of social commitments, responsibilities and engagement.

You are wary of anyone making you responsible for their feelings, decisions and wellbeing. In close relationships, you easily feel smothered or imposed upon by the needs of others. You may hold back from showing affection and approval to your partner and children, suggesting they should be able to support themselves without your constant reassurance. You have little tolerance for conflicts and heated emotions; when someone confronts you, you 'cut off' by turning your gaze away, keeping your head down and diverting attention.[13] You may use avoidant strategies such as silent treatment, deflecting the subject, rationalizing your behaviours, or escaping into work. Your partner complains about your withholding pattern, but the more they push you, the more you pull back.

To maintain emotional distance, you have turned the rest of humanity into what feels like a subject matter or a system that you can study. In social occasions, you take a 'helicopter view' and dispassionately watch the world go by. In group settings, you find a way to hide, to deflect attention, and to shift the spotlight onto someone else.

Emotional and intimacy anorexia

Having 'emotional anorexia' means you struggle or refuse to take in the necessary nourishment from love and kinship. When people show you affection in various forms – ranging from compliments, concern, friendship and help, to erotic desires – you cannot trust it or take it in. On a deep level, you fear manipulation.

You worry that once you are 'hooked', you will be used or will become over-committed. So you would rather remain in a state of emotional deprivation than take the risk. As opposed to having no or loose personal boundaries, the line you draw between yourself and others is rigid and inflexible. You hardly give people a chance to prove themselves worthy of trust and tend to reject them pre-emptively. You may appear to be open to relationships but, on close examination, you choose to be with people who are out of reach or not ready for emotional closeness. On the other hand, if you repeatedly dismiss or invalidate the positive feelings others have towards you, people with genuine intent may stop approaching you for friendships, and you may be left with only distant or unhealthy relationships in your life.

The distance you keep with the rest of humanity keeps you disconnected, not just socially but also spiritually. The more you believe you have to 'go it on your own', the more you compulsively accumulate knowledge and resources. You focus on experiences that escalate your distrust, and collect more and more evidence to justify your isolation. You may not notice your own attachment needs or the impact of your seclusion. From time to time, however, you experience a sudden worsening of your mental health or nihilistic feelings towards life. You may be a high achiever in the professional arena or appear successful, independent and self-contained, but inside you battle with perfectionism, shame, and loneliness. In the long run, intimacy anorexia is counter-productive. As you shrink your social life and the capacity to connect, you also curtail how far you can go in life. Gradually, your days become one-dimensional and sterile, with little vitality and room for growth.

Cutting off from emotions

You were a highly empathic kid, but your sensitivity might have been abused rather than honoured. It is not surprising that to protect yourself, you have learned to do the opposite of being sensitive: to stop feeling. Your parents were the only people you depended on as a child; even if they were neglectful, punitive or abusive, you did not have the resources to seek refuge. You were trapped, and dissociation became the escape when there was no escape. In psychology, the term 'dissociation' describes a spectrum of experiences from mild disconnection from your surroundings to a more severe detachment from your physical body and emotional reality. It sometimes involves minimizing a painful past or selectively forgetting parts of your early life. You may use substances or addictive behaviours as a part of your dissociative strategies. Eating, alcohol, compulsive behaviours and repetitive rituals can become addictive because they function to fill an inner void.

As you cut off from yourself, you also lose connection with your body and intuition. You may experience surreal experiences of a mind–body split. For example, in certain situations your mind says you are calm, but you are trembling and sweating and getting a headache. Or, you tell yourself that you 'should' be a loyal friend and lover, and a diligent worker, while your depression and irritations speak the opposite.

The more you avoid getting in touch with your true feelings, the more you feel like an observer of life, watching as it goes by in front of you without being part of it. Ironically, the deep sadness and loneliness that comes from such a non-living state can be as painful as, if not more painful than the original emotional turmoil that you were trying to avoid. Running away from the 'hotness' of emotions in the moment, you end up in a dry, cold, and arid land that is indeed no better than the original struggle.

Intellectualizing

To stay sane in your childhood environment, you might have tried various means. If your environment was chaotic and your parents were unpredictable, the predictability and consistency of logic offered an alluring refuge. The 'flight into reason' quickly became your default coping mechanism, but you paid the hefty price of losing touch with your emotions. You may talk about strong feelings like anger in a distant, logical way ('I guess in theory, I should be angry about that'), or have a habit of rationalizing your experience.

When you overly rely on your intellect, you start to struggle with endeavours that call for playfulness, humour or artistic expressions.[14] To avoid the feelings of being out of control, you rehearse every situation in your mind before taking action, and feel you have to gather enough information before saying anything. You may be able to maintain a calm, collected and intelligent demeanour, but you are not able to be spontaneous, freely express yourself or relax into the company of others.

Initially, hiding in your head seems helpful – it helps you to show up to work with a stoic outlook and to achieve tangible goals in the world. In the long run, however, over-intellectualizing everything is like only using only one crayon to draw a picture, instead of using the whole spectrum of colours. It limits your human potential, and has a detrimental impact on your ability to be effective in the world.

Excessive daydreaming

Another dimension of hiding in your head is excessive daydreaming. As a child in an unpredictable environment, the only thing under your control was your imagination. You created elaborate other-worlds that you preferred to live in, and when it became extreme, you avoided life altogether. This act of turning inward and retreating into your own world can become addictive. Once you have at your disposal a readily available, instantly gratifying means for mitigating stress and numbing emotional pain, it becomes comfortable and familiar. What once was a survival mechanism may now remain in you as an addictive habit pattern. Rather than facing the chaos of relationships in real life, you spend a large part of your waking life in fantasies.

Can you find your way back?

Survival strategies such as counter-dependency, intellectualizing and emotional anorexia were once essential for the survival of your psyche; they justified the unbearable pain in your early life and helped to protect your young mind from annihilating despair. However, when these strategies overstay their time and become the only ways you know, they can hold you back from living a full life. If your early experience of life has not made you feel safe, it is difficult for you to believe that things could be any different. Even when circumstances change, you may continue to live in a cage that your mind has created. Your fear of intimacy sets up a vicious cycle: you have built such thick walls to protect the tenderness in you, but the more you defend against the world, the more fragile you feel on the inside. Because you have not built up the necessary tolerance for the ebbs and flows of relationships, you become hyper-sensitized to the pain of potential rejection and misunderstanding; eventually, you become inept at relating to others. Buried underneath the aloof facade, however, is a deeply sensitive and passionate heart; it was forced into hiding but has not gone away. Your buried longing for love and connection may persistently knock on your door in the forms of unnamed melancholy, nostalgia, and heartache. Without a means of expression, your frustration will fester into depression.

The answer to healing from defensive non-attachment is to build trust in your inner resources. You pushed away love because you feared you could not survive more intrusion and betrayal, and therefore to break through you must first reassure the scared child inside of you of his or her safety. As an adult, the basis of your ability to trust and to love does not lie in the hands of others but in your own resilience. Yes, people may irritate, disappoint, or betray you, but these feelings do not have to traumatize you. You can grieve, be angry, live through the hurt, and bounce back from it. You are not blind to the ever-changing nature of reality, or the dark side of human nature, but you are brave enough to dive into life itself.

To go from surviving to thriving, you must stretch your comfort zone. You can start dissolving the armour you built by getting comfortable with the feeling of tenderness. Rather than insisting on having absolute control, practise relaxing into the flux of life. All relationships in life involve uncertainty; and the more intimate they are, the more vulnerable you feel. However, this vulnerability is not weakness, but a sign of courage. As a sensitive person in a relationship, some days are harder than others. At times, you feel more tender, more porous, and more affected by every little blow. However, even during your bleakest hours, see if you can suspend your judgement on people and events, and take a pause to see reality clearly. People and your feelings towards them are not here to haunt you, but rather they are invitations for you to process and digest what was unfinished so that you can become more whole, more healed, and free. Our ability to love and risk being loved is the most tender, yet strongest, part of our human capacity and the origin of much of our creative potential.

> Falling in love and becoming attached to another is one of the most intense, enriching and exuberant experiences of human life. Do not deprive yourself of the sweetness of intimacy, the joy of finding belongingness in another's heart, and the ecstasy of discovering yourself in their eyes.

Week-long journaling exercise: is your avoidance working for you?

For the next week, set the intention to reflect on your potential tendency to avoid intimacy. With your journal, use the following questions and prompts to guide your process.

1 What pushes you to the edge?

Intimacy can feel like a threat to your system because it asks you to relinquish your need to control, and reveals the parts of you that you would rather deny or hide. It invites you to penetrate deeply into your shadows and to invoke the rawest true self. When you welcome someone new into your life, you are challenged to process your dormant wounds, and step into unknown territories.

Depending on your personality and past experience, the triggers for your urge to withdraw are unique to you. For this week, pay close attention to your inner experience as you interact with others. Notice the moments where you feel stirred up. Observe how you feel when, for example, you have an argument with someone close to you. As these occasions occur, make notes in your phone or a notebook. When you are emotionally triggered, what thoughts do you have? How does your body react to these experiences? What do you tend to say or do in response to the other person?

At the end of the week, review what you have recorded. Then see if the situations in question tend to fall into one or more of the following categories. This exercise helps you to reflect on the relational themes that trigger strong emotional reactions in you, or cause you to retreat from others:

- Feeling controlled
- Being pressured to commit
- Being dragged into a conflict

- Feeling engulfed or smothered
- Someone touching you without your permission
- Someone moving your property without asking
- Being put on the spot to answer questions
- Being pressed to take a definitive stance on something
- Someone making decisions for you, or speaking on your behalf
- You suspect that you have been lied to, manipulated, deceived
- Having to collaborate with someone
- Having to negotiate on personal space
- Having to provide emotional support to someone
- Having to disclose intimate details about your life
- Being asked to give honest feedback on someone or something
- Someone not respecting your time, or the potential of losing your own time.

You may add your own items to the list.

2 What strategies do you use to evade closeness or to cope with difficult situations in relationships?

Using the notes you have made this week, reflect on any conscious or unconscious methods you have used to cope with challenging feelings that have arisen in relationships.

Some examples may be:

- Distracting yourself
- Mentally checking out
- Escaping into reminiscing about the past, daydreaming or making lofty goals
- Intellectualizing and rationalizing
- Numbing out feelings
- Changing subjects in conversation

- Pretending that you are listening to pacify others
- Work excessively or use busy-ness as an excuse to disengage
- Giving your partner the silent-treatment or cold shoulder
- Burying your head in the sand when it comes to conflicts
- Using substances such as drugs, alcohol, or excessive sugar to numb out feelings
- Over-spending, gambling
- Compulsive cleaning
- Engaging in rigid rituals and routines.

You may add your own items to the list.

3 How have these methods worked in your favour?

You have used these strategies because they have worked. For at least a while, they have helped you to reduce, escape or get rid of negative feelings. Make a list of ways in which these strategies have served you.

For example, your strategies have:

- Allowed you to show up to work even when you were having a bad day
- Helped you to get through a painful breakup
- Protected your inner child from more disappointments
- Defended you against controlling and engulfing parents
- Helped you to survive a childhood environment that was chaotic and unpredictable
- Allowed you to appear strong to fit into a particular peer or work culture
- Helped you to behave in socially approved ways.

You may add your own items to the list.

After you have made the list, respectfully thank your defence mechanisms, and congratulate yourself for being able to come up with these creative ways to cope. Acknowledge that you did the best you could with all that you had, and that they have served you for as long as you had needed them to.

4 What consequences have these strategies brought?

Your strategies have worked for at least a while, but they often come with an expiry date, do not work in some circumstances, or come with a hefty cost. Enter into a quiet space and reflect candidly on the following questions:

- Are your strategies sustainable?
- When you use an avoidant strategy, for how long do you feel the relief?
- Do the unpleasant feelings eventually come back?
- How much time and energy does it take to keep the strategies going?
- What do you miss out on by isolating yourself, avoiding emotional exchange, or keeping busy?
- Will your future self thank you for avoiding intimacy?
- If you were to take a longer view, has your life become better or worse?
- How may you better invest the time and energy that you have used to sustain your flight from intimacy?

If some of these methods do indeed work in the long run, please by all means keep them. However, if some of them look like they work only for a short while or cost you dearly in other ways, you may want to consider if there are other methods that will help you feel safe, well, and whole in the longer term.

5 Imagery exercise: speaking with your wall

Set aside at least half an hour for this self-guided visualization exercise.

Imagine that there is a part within you that is trying so hard to keep you safe from getting hurt; you can call it a manager, a shield, a wall or a protector. This part of you tries to control everything, from external circumstances to your inner world. This is the 'doer' in you who pushes you to achieve more, strive more and be chronically busy. Whenever soft emotions or vulnerable feelings emerge in you, it kicks in to dampen, suppress and push them down – leaving you withdrawn, distracted, depersonalized and empty.

Imagine this part of you is a person. What might they look like? Is this person a he or a she? Does their voice remind you of someone in your life? Roughly how old are they?

Sit down with this person who has protected you for all these years, and ask them the following questions. Write the answers in your journal.

- For how long now have you been with me?
- Who or what are you trying to protect me from?
- How have your strategies evolved throughout the years?
- If you were not here, what do you think would happen to me?
- Do you feel angry towards people, or the way things are in the world?
- Do you feel sad that shielding me is the only thing you can do to protect me?
- Deep down, do you feel alone and misunderstood?
- Do you feel tired, after all these years of defending me?
- Are there times where you would like to take a break, or try something different?

Thank, honour and validate your protector for all they have done for you.

Now, see if you can convince them to consider stepping aside from the centre of your life. You may want to reassure them that although you were once vulnerable, you are now much more resilient, and can deal with disappointments, heartbreaks and hurt in life. Let them know that throughout the years, you have learned what your rights are, what healthy boundaries look like, how to say no, and how to express your wants and needs. You are no longer naive, and although people can be unreliable and relationships are sometimes messy, you are capable of handling them. You are not completely letting go of your protector, but inviting them to take a short break, so you can experiment with a different way of being, and to grow in life.

As you try to dissolve an armour that has been with you for a long time, there may be sadness, anger, grief or guilt. Notice the feelings that show up at this juncture, and try to breathe softly with any resistant feelings you have.

For the next week or so, notice the occasions where you feel your protector coming into play. Then, see if you can experiment with a different behaviour. Make a note of how it feels, and pay attention to the sense of empowerment and hope that comes from taking courageous and life-giving actions.

7
Work relationships and friendships

When you work in an organization, your work life involves complex group dynamics that could be a source of both nourishment and destruction. Our experiences of being and working in groups are powerful, as they heighten many of our internal battles. In institutional life, we come face to face with the tension between togetherness and independence, group identity and separateness, collectivist values and individualism. Being a non-conformist in groups also thrusts us into our deepest fears of either engulfment, or of being outcast and ostracized.

Understanding workplace challenges

Like individuals, institutions have unconscious defence mechanisms in place to deal with feelings or subjects that are either too threatening or too painful to deal with. These mechanisms, known as social defence mechanisms, may include denial, splitting, idealization and blame. They may also include external projection – where a group of people actively dislodge what they cannot face in order to avoid the need to address it. While they are mostly unnamed and invisible, these group dynamics create a myriad of complex problems for the intense person.

In this chapter, we will review some of the common problems you may face in a workplace. Until you can see the issues lucidly, you may continue to confuse the personal with the systemic, and take what is a natural reaction to toxic infiltration as an individual defect. It is my hope that this information will provide you with a new perspective.

Being too much and not enough

As an intense person, you are considered to be both 'too much' in some areas and 'not enough' in others. Your brain operates like a fast car, and naturally you have a strong drive that propels you to take actions. When you are engaged, you may become hyper-focused on a subject or project and are unable to relax, even after work. Your imagination stretches far beyond the natural confines; you see patterns and trends that are ahead of your time and most people cannot keep up with your foresight. Not understanding your intensity, others may say your energy is 'too much' and mock your efforts. You naturally give a lot of yourself; you may find yourself working harder than everyone else but are still not appreciated, and are continuously picking up the slack for others. What seems normal to you may be idealistic to others, which puts you in a lonely battle for excellence. Since your work ethics raise the standards for everyone else, those who are managed by you may resent the pressure to perform. With little support for your skills and efficiency, you are left feeling stifled and exploited.

Paradoxically, you might be criticized for not being energized, invested or interested enough when social convention requires you to be. While you thrive in meaningful conversations and can have intellectually stimulating debates at length, you are not interested in small talk, gossip, drunk talk and water-cooler chitchat. Your energy plummets in networking events, parties, or mundane meetings. Even though you know that a diplomatic facade may be necessary, you struggle to sustain interest. Most of the time, you cannot hide your restlessness and impatience. You may have to doodle, daydream or fidget in order to cope, but these can be seen as disrespectful by your colleagues and seniors.

Being burned out and bored out

Another conundrum you face is that of being simultaneously burned out and bored out. On the one hand, your physical body is overloaded by sensory input from a modern workplace. You do not feel at ease in a chaotic, noisy, open workspace with machines, typing sounds, bright fluorescent light and people murmuring in the background. Apart from these sensory stimulants, your empathic nature causes you to pick up on people's emotional energy. All the time, you detect relationship dynamics and changes in the atmosphere. All these can overload your system, hamper your productivity, and lead to burn out. While you can use small tools such as earplugs or headphones to help, the traditional work culture is not usually understanding or able to cater to your needs.

Although you are physically burned out, you may be intellectually, emotionally and spiritually under-stimulated. Given your multiple interests, you may not be able to sustain a narrow-focus even a specialized work role requires you to. Monetary reward alone is insufficient to motivate you, and you crave a more profound – more spiritual – purpose. You feel a hunger for more knowledge and the need for a soul-search, but you are weighed down by tedious, repetitive, and meaningless tasks. You seek new challenges and problems to stay engaged, but your zeal may be mistaken as competitiveness. Given the depth of your thinking and the complexity of your mental processes, it is not easy to find intellectual equals to share or bounce ideas off. Chronic under-stimulation leads to 'bore-out', which will leave you feeling depressed, empty, and resentful.

You absorb the feelings that others dislodge

Among the multitude of social defence mechanisms, collective denial is common in both large and small organizations. Through denial, people push certain thoughts, feelings and experiences out of their conscious awareness because they are simply too unsettling and take them too far out of their comfort zone. Common subjects that are pushed down due to the anxiety that they generate include workplace bullying, discrimination, power harassment, and uncertainty about prospective lay-off. Suppression of anxiety and anger associated with these issues is often reinforced via 'group-think', systemic oppression, and even ideological indoctrination.

As an empath, however, denial is not a part of your natural defence. Instead, you likely absorb and feel the very emotion that the group has denied, suppressed, or disowned. For example, at a critical business juncture where the whole company faces potential disintegration and financial uncertainty, you may find yourself to be the only person feeling depressed and anxious. Or, as you are infuriated by a blatantly abusive situation, you are struck by how indifferent your colleagues appear. As you feel emotions on behalf of the group, you also serve as a sponge for all the anger, grief, guilt and despair that they have systemically dislodged.

Usually, you are not aware of your role as the emotional 'sponge'. Rather, you think the disturbing emotions – especially rage – belong to you. You may have assumed you were 'just too sensitive' or were 'imagining things' but, if you can understand these hidden psychodynamics, you will come to see that your salient feelings offer important information about what is truly going on beneath the surface at your workplace. If harnessed correctly, your empathic skills and astute observations may be exactly the change agent that the organization needs.

You ask the difficult questions

Most people in large organizations do not dare to upset the equilibrium, and will instead turn a blind eye to any problems, and opt for passivity. They look to a leader to devise actions, and see themselves as mere followers. Instead of contemplating ideas that initiate systemic changes, most people think only on a local level. Out of fear, they exert most of their energy in avoiding mistakes or conflicts, rather than thinking of ways to improve things. Even when they witness injustice, instead of naming what is clearly going wrong, they resort only to rumours and silent protests. Their unspoken agreement to remain silent may provide a false sense of togetherness, yet such complacency only perpetuates a rigid and dysfunctional system.

Your ability to think independently, combined with your drive towards autonomous actions, makes you an outlier to the system. Most likely, you are the one who is awake in an environment where most are asleep. It does not escape your radar when people are acting in unfair or unethical ways. Because doing your work well is more important to you than pleasing others, you don't mind asking difficult questions if it means improving the integrity of your work.

What you may not see is that you are unconsciously being placed by the group dynamic to perform a unique function. Implicitly, you are 'voted up' to be the questioner and the challenger, who now carries the responsibility of having to confront the authorities who said the wrong things, of holding individuals accountable, of upholding the moral principles for a committee, or of drawing attention to a critical flaw that would otherwise be missed. Because you are expressing doubts and frustrations on behalf of your colleagues, they do not have to. They may sit awkwardly with you in the same room, exchanging facial expressions with each other that signal their dismay, while secretly enjoying not having to take a risk to expose themselves. Conveniently, they have outsourced the expression of anger and doubt to you, so that you can act as a mouthpiece for the group.

Your colleagues hold a conflicting love–hate relationship about your presence. Unconsciously, they are relieved by your presence, as without you the issue will never come to the surface. At the same time, they fear the change you will bring to the system. They secretly benefit from your honesty but fear your perceptiveness. It can become all too easy for others to continue to frame your directness, assertiveness and forthrightness as undesirable defects, while paradoxically depending on you to express what is suppressed, balance what is imbalanced, and regulate what is out-of-order. Unfortunately, until other members of the group are able to step up to own their voice, you may continue to be outcast as the 'troublemaker' or 'the difficult one'.

You have all the responsibilities but none of the power

Many intense people are stuck in an 'impossible middle' in their workplace. Because you are a fast learner, you acquire skills with little effort. Inevitably, your colleagues come to rely on your competence and efficiency. Although unspoken, you are regarded as a leader and have to shoulder heavy responsibilities, but often you are not given the acknowledgement or rewards that you deserve.

Rather than being driven by external recognition, your motivation with work is most likely intrinsic. You strive for excellence because you enjoy the thrill of being challenged, excelling at a task and meeting your own standards. This means you are not normally in a race to fame. Even though power is not your primary driver, it is still important for you to attain the recognition you deserve, and the freedom that comes with a legitimate position. Autonomy is required for your creative mind to thrive. When you are stuck in a semi-senior, middle-management position where you are micromanaged, you are burdened by bureaucracy but deprived of the space to make your creative vision come true.

You may face hindrances in gaining what you deserve due to envy. On the one hand, the ones seniors to you count on you for your productivity and creativity, but they are also intimidated by your speed, insight, and intelligence. They may delegate task after task to you, but are reluctant to share their power. To get the resources and information you need, you have to 'manage your manager'. Unfortunately, it is often difficult to provide evidence for the silent oppression you face. Others are likely to turn a blind eye to it, which perpetuates the injustice of the situation.

The ultimate exile – becoming the target of splitting

As a defence mechanism, splitting is defined as the polarization of beliefs, actions, objects or persons into good and bad by focusing selectively on their positive or negative attributes. Splitting was first described by psychoanalyst Ronald Fairbairn.[1] It begins as the inability of the infant to combine their parents' fulfilling aspects (the good) and their disappointing aspects (the bad) into an integrated whole. It is natural for a child to see things in black and white because the young mind is not developed enough to handle complexities. This is why in children's literature, there are distinctive characters such as the good fairy godmother and the wicked witch. When someone or something is split into the 'good' camp, they are idealized as the one who can do no wrong. If someone is rendered as 'bad', they are framed as the cause of all troubles and difficulties. As a child, we use splitting as a way of making sense of the world, to gain relief from confusion and to retain a sense of control. Grown-ups under stress can regress, and resort to using splitting in order to deal with anxieties and conflicts. Institutional dilemmas such as staying stagnant versus the need to change, or discrimination versus justice, are anxiety-provoking, and regularly give rise to splitting. Tensions embedded on a systemic level get played out between individuals or sub-groups. Tribes are formed to bolster a sense of identity and offer people a false sense of reassurance. Usually, a me-versus-them scenario is created: if the people in

Camp A are to be blamed then, by implication, the people in Camp B are not, and could therefore be the ones who either point fingers or sit back in self-satisfaction.[2]

A person is vulnerable to being the target of splitting when they are an outsider. For example, a new employee or an external consultant often gets labelled as the enemy. But it also happens when you are in a minority, such as being one who out-performs, the introvert in an extraverted culture, the one who speaks up when others do not. Within a system, intense people tend to sit on the fringe. You are a part of the institution. But clearly, in terms of the way you think, feel, and behave, and the qualities you represent, you are not fully a part of the crowd. Being on the border immediately casts you in the role of 'the other', rendering you the target of splitting, as well as receiving projections of hatred and enmity.[3]

Given the current climate of economic uncertainty and shrinking budgets, survival anxiety is amplified, which encourages the tendency to resort to primitive defence mechanisms such as splitting. Unfortunately, splitting sets up a negative cycle that perpetuates itself. Staff members with individual defences that align with the institution's social defence systems tend to stay. While those whose values are out of sync with the institution's stagnation are ostracized or pushed to the edges. While the denial of healthy change is not ultimately conducive to a healthy organization, this unfortunately is what often happens.[4] When you are scapegoated, the value of your work is automatically diminished. Even though your insights may be exactly what the organization needs, they are readily discarded. At the extreme end of splitting, you may be asked to leave your job, or even get bullied out of it, despite your many contributions.

Embrace your destiny

Sensitive and intense people are knowledge seekers, truth-tellers, and idealists. All your life, you may have felt like someone who is on the outside looking in, or that you were never able to fit in or be part of a group like others were. You felt as though you were a Martian on Earth or a wizard outside of Hogwarts. You cannot change who you are, but you can embrace your traits and make the best of them. By learning to do so, you move from a place of powerlessness to strength, from feeling like a victim to having gratitude for who you are.

One of the essential steps to embracing your destiny is to grieve the life that you wish you had. We know how to grieve actual losses of people and things, but we can also grieve the ideal lives we always wanted but could never have. You may never be able to fit in in an ordinary way. You may never be able to identify with mainstream values or tolerate the mundane activities others seem to enjoy. You may always feel out of sync. However, once you realize who you are, you let go of certain hopes and dreams and liberate yourself from the ideals that you could never attain.

Our culture and society celebrate sameness, and it takes inner strength and practice to be comfortable with not being the 'norm'. You will find tremendous relief and peace if you can stop trying to be what you are not. Just because others reject you doesn't make you wrong. You are different, and that doesn't make you defective in any way. It does mean that you need to be better equipped for the bruises and attacks life has in store for you, though. It may make you scream again and again that life is unfair, but life has never promised fairness. What it does promise, though, is that you will find joy and fulfilment by growing into who you are.

The answer to thriving in any workplace is not to avoid difficulties, but to build strengths and develop strategies so you can thrive even in challenging circumstances. You cannot stop others from attacking or oppressing you at work, but it is in your power to manage your reaction. In the next chapter, we will discuss how we can manage criticism and rejection, set boundaries, and turn hostile situations into opportunities to learn and grow.

Exploration: what are your roles?

Sometimes, the workplace can feel like a theatre stage on which we play out our individual and collective psychodrama. From a system perspective, different members of the group must have designated tasks for the operation to function. Sometimes these roles are fluid and dynamic, at other times they can become rigid and fixed. Reflecting on the archetypal role/roles you play within a system can help you assess your place in the group, and how it fits in with your personality.

Identify under which circumstances, or in what ways, you play the following roles when you are at work:

I play the role of 'the caregiver' when I _____.

I play the role of 'the joker' when I _____.

I play the role of 'the creative' when I _____.

I play the role of 'the wise sage' when I _____.

I play the role of 'the ruler' when I _____.

I play the role of 'the hero' when I _____.

I play the role of 'the mediator' when I _____.

I play the role of 'the problem solver' when I _____.

Which roles do you enjoy playing, and which roles do you resent having to play?

Under which role/roles is your intensity put into its best use?

Do you tend to fall into particular roles most of the time? Are there certain roles that you have come to identify strongly with? Do these roles authentically reflect your personality? Do you gladly step into them, or are they imposed upon you? How do they impact your work performance or your sense of fulfilment at work?

Has your workplace become a replica of the way these roles were enacted in your family?

If it was up to you, what role/roles would you rather play more?

Thriving at work

It is not uncommon for an intense person to feel like a frustrated outlier at work. Perhaps you thrive in the technical or intellectual parts of your work but struggle to navigate the complex webs of relationships and power dynamics. It can be that you enjoy dealing with clients and customers, but not your colleagues and manager. There is no mentor to support your growth or offer you guidance. Worse, those in higher positions are intimidated by you. Those you manage cannot keep up with your standards and say you are unnecessarily serious. Maybe your strengths are not seen, and your contributions are dismissed. You can see loopholes and dysfunctions in the system, but your voice is oppressed by authorities that you do not respect.

Sometimes, you cannot help but be the whistleblower, but that is seldom a welcome move. With the absence of an ethical or empathic culture, or true peers who share your values, you may feel sidelined, alone and unsupported.

Rising above your workplace challenges

With all the time and effort you have invested, it is understandable that you want to feel appreciated and supported in your workplace. You may have adapted yourself to fit in, and temporarily you have been able to find a sense of kinship. Unfortunately, by editing and silencing yourself, you can only arrive at a false sense of belonging. If you settle for being tolerated instead of seeking places where you will be celebrated, you may just one day realize the only thing that fitted in was your facade.

While a supportive workplace would be ideal, it is not always possible to make a career move. When you are confronted by a challenging day-to-day environment, the answer is not to escape or to hide, but to have mental strategies that deal with the challenges that come your way. The following are some pointers that may be helpful if you find yourself in a work environment that does not appreciate the gifts of your intensity.

Recognize the times when you have time-travelled

When you are stressed and unsupported at work, you may find that even the slightest signal of rejection or criticism can send you in an emotional downward spiral. What triggers this may appear minor – someone looks away or interrupts you, or you are uncertain about what is on their mind.

Instinctively, you may beat yourself up for having extreme reactions, but having emotional flashbacks is not something that you can consciously control. The hurt you feel does not come from your adult self but rather the child inside you. Your inner child is the child you once were – the child who was innocent but vulnerable. They might have been wounded, threatened or isolated. These situations bring back the early memories that hurt you the most; perhaps you have always been dismissed by your siblings, your teacher did not take you seriously, or your parents always cut you off when you were about to say something. They may also represent some of your lifelong battles, such as others not getting where you are coming from, not being able to keep up with you, or projecting negative qualities onto you. What is happening now leads your memory system to release all the locked-up images of being misunderstood, bullied and alienated. As your fight–flight system gets activated, the amygdala (the part of your brain responsible for your emotions) hijacks the rational part of the brain and blocks your capacity for reasoning. Even though the adult, logical part of you knows that other people's disapproval of you can do no real damage, you still feel your body and psyche crumbling due to past trauma. In other words, you have temporarily lost touch with your actual reality, and have mentally 'time-travelled' to the past.

What has made you especially vulnerable to being triggered might be your unconscious expectation for work colleagues to treat you the way a loving family would. Perhaps you desperately need recognition from authority figures because that was what you had wanted from your parents; you crave closeness with your colleagues because that was missing among your siblings as you were growing up. Rightly so, your inner child wants love and approval. Unfortunately, the workplace is rarely the place for your emotional needs to be met.

Instead of blaming yourself further for your suffering, you can make conscious efforts to separate your current reality from your past memories. The first step is to become aware of them as flashbacks happen. Then, remind yourself that, although your feelings are real, they do not always reflect your current reality. Just because you feel like a helpless five-year-old with no place to turn to and no one to support you, it does not mean that is the truth. You may say to yourself, 'The worst has already happened. This flashback will pass as it has many times before.' You are now a strong adult who can walk away, stand up for yourself and solicit help. With practice, you can become your best possible friend, mentor and protector. You can whisper to your wounded inner child to soothe their fears. You can create an imaginary safe cradle for them. You reaffirm the fact that no matter what happens there is no reason for them to feel shame or guilt. They have not done anything wrong and, even though bad things happen, it is not their fault. Eventually, your inner child will learn that you are their source of love and support and will no longer seek it from the outside.

The integration with your inner child may be just what you need to thrive at work. After all, the best leaders are those who retain the spontaneity and humility of a child but walk into the boardroom with the resilience and maturity of an adult.

See projections clearly

If you come away from a situation feeling sad, angry or resentful, it is a sign that your boundaries have been compromised. Your boundaries are what protects your emotional health. Sensitive and highly reflective people tend to take on too many responsibilities for what happens in a relationship, and allow other people's unprocessed psychological materials to not only exhaust their energy but also erode their self-image. To change this pattern, you can learn to develop boundaries that are flexible but not porous, so you can draw a line between your psyche and others telling you what emotional materials belong to you and what you are not accountable for.

To find your boundaries, it is useful to have some understanding of common group dynamics and behaviours, and what people consciously or unconsciously do in situations where they are confronted with differences. Many of the common large-group dynamics, including the human tendency to project insecurities and frustrations outward, are laid out in the previous chapter. It is crucial that you can identify other people's hostility as what it is, especially when it is disguised as passive-aggressive comments and actions. When you live an authentic but counter-normative life, others may not know where to 'place you'. To those who conform, your actions are too progressive, too rebellious, too daring. They are bothered by not being able to neatly fit you into a category in their mind. Maybe you act out what they did not dare to feel, voice, or do. If what you stand for threatens their existing worldview or their choices, they may cope with their anxiety by oppressing your voice. This is when they say you are being 'aggressive' for being honest, call you a 'drama queen' for your sensitivity, or name you the 'trouble-maker' for your moral integrity.

Bear in mind that most criticisms and name-calling come from a place of fear – from people's own internal struggles, insecurities, jealousy and general inability to hold multiple perspectives. What you felt as a rejection was not a rejection of you and your real essence, but a product of their limited perspective. The attacks you experience are the result of another person not being able to bear their inner tension or ambiguity. As much as you can, remember that most of the time, other people's opinion of you has very little to do with who you are.

Make room for a healthy push back

When someone violates your boundaries, anger, resentment and bitterness are normal emotional reactions. As we have seen previously, anger is a messenger that comes and warns you when what you value is compromised. Since anger has important functions, suppressing it may cause you to become confused about your place in the world – who you are, your values, what you believe in, and what your rights are. When someone mistreats you, instead of crumbling in helplessness, or reacting to violence with violence, you can summon healthy assertiveness to stand up for yourself and resume your rights. It takes some practice, but you can learn to push back on injustice without hurting yourself or others.

Over the course of your day, be aware of any run-up to the energy of resentment, so you can be mindful of and manage it promptly. As irritation, annoyance or impatience emerges, shift your attention away from the ceaseless mental chatter, and drop into your body. Pay close attention to the pure sensation the situation has created, such as heat, contraction, and tightness. With simple strategies such as counting from 1 to 10 or breathing deeply, buy as much time as you possibly can, and try not to act out of the immediate, primal fight-or-flight response, or say things you will regret. If possible, disengage from a situation and cool off. Simply witness how these sensations rise and fall within you, and notice that if you stop pouring gasoline on the fire with mental loops or further grievance, they will soon cease without causing any harm. Being able to witness your bodily sensations brings you a space between stimulus and response, and it is in this space that you can decide the best course of action.

Once the first wave of 'hot emotions' has passed, you have an opportunity to harness your resentment as a healing and growing opportunity. Carefully examine the unmet needs that are driving the bitterness or the urge to take revenge – was your safety, right to expressions or dignity harmed in any way? Without being carried away by a sense of righteous indignation or denying all feelings of vulnerability, allow yourself to drop into the tender spots within you. Then, turn towards the hurting, fearful one within you and imagine standing up for them. If you struggle to come up with what to say or do next, imagine having someone you trust coming in – what might they say or do on your behalf? If you were a child and the most powerful, intelligent adult comes to your rescue, how might they react? What can you do now, to meet the needs that have been deprived? Although you cannot control how others behave, you have the power to guard your mental, physical and psychic boundaries. With practice, healthy assertiveness can become the portal to your vitality, creativity and all the elements that are essential to your thriving at work.

Anchor yourself

When you are triggered, it is easy to get into a collapsed state and allow one unpleasant experience to take over your entire reality. This happens because you are in shock and your fight/flight/freeze system gets activated, and you are having a nauseating upside-down flip of perception. However, if you can take a step back and look at the full picture, you will see that the interpersonal injury, however painful, is not pervasive.

The times when you feel the most vulnerable are the golden opportunities for you to practise drawing strength from your inner and outer resources. Your inner resources may be your values, work ethics, past positive experiences and resilience. Your outer resources may be your mentor, friends, people who love you, and institutions that value your input. Although positive experiences do not replace the negative ones, one person's disapproval of you does not have to bleed into all other areas of your life. Even amidst difficult circumstances, see if you can bring into mind experiences of love, gratitude, creativity and connection – and allow them to be the basis of your sense of fulfilment. Anchoring yourself is not just an intellectual exercise, but an embodied experience through which you make the message 'I am a lovable, worthy, dignified human being' a part of your inner reality.

To do this, neuropsychologist Rick Hanson suggests that we make a conscious effort to internalize positive and loving everyday experiences. When you feel love, confidence and dignity, reinforce the positive neuro-pathways by taking five or ten (or more) seconds to protect and stay with these experiences. You can intentionally prolong and intensify them, and try to remember how they make you feel, both in your mind and in your body. The more these good feelings are reinforced, the more you are 'wiring' inner strength into your brain, and they will form the source of your self-reliance, emotional balance and confidence.

Another useful reminder when you are in the midst of a toxic environment is that however unpleasant, these experiences are not permanent. When your feelings are taking over, be mindful of thoughts that involve words such as 'always' and 'never' as they can reinforce a rigid storyline and breed feelings of powerlessness and hopelessness. Ask yourself: will anyone care about this in the future? Will it matter in five or ten years' time? Any moment gives you an opportunity to change your story, and there is no 'rest of my life' and no 'for years'. It hurts, and it passes. When it does, you will still be standing firm in your integrity.

Be a participant-observer

One of the most effective mental strategies when it comes to dealing with a toxic or misaligned work environment is to practise becoming a mindful observer. You can put on a scientist's hat or think of yourself as an anthropologist. Anthropologists live with people of the culture they are studying. They eat with them, spend time with them, ask questions and reflect on their interactions. They are participants as much as they are observers.

As an anthropologist, you are present in your work life, learning and observing, but you are not entangled with what you witness. To start, you can imagine taking a 'helicopter view' of what is going on, and make a note of how other people's behaviours play out in a way that is not personal to you. Then, draw an imaginary line between your own energetic and psychological space and their hostile energies. This line is your boundary. With some distance, you also free up the capacity for compassion. You will see that underneath people's aggression are their wounds, pain, and vulnerability. You can then say, 'Isn't it interesting that this is how humans work – they project things outward.' Having healthy boundaries allows you to feel safe and resilient, so you can love and give without worrying about depletion, be kind to others without excessive care-taking, and forgive those who have wronged you without disowning your power.

You can also have a ritual to mark a role switch between your 'real self' and your 'work self'. For example, as you get dressed in the morning, imagine putting on a suit of armour. You will be an actor or actress, playing a role in the workplace. No matter what happens then, take any projection or criticism that is directed your way and imagine it not as directed towards you but, rather, the character you play. As you come home from work, you can take off the shield, and your real self remains untethered. By separating yourself from other people's toxic projections and mental drama, you can send them good thoughts and blessings for the pain and suffering you witness.

Finding your place in the world

To be both authentic and find belongingness in the world, you must learn to hold various paradoxes.

- People can be disappointing, but they can change and surprise you at any time.

- You are different to others, but you are also interconnected.
- You can have judgements, but you reserve the right to change your mind.
- People can be hypocritical and act aggressively, but this does not capture all of who they are.
- At times, you may edit yourself just to stay safe in the social arena but, at other times, you must open your door and enjoy letting others in to receive your full, buoyant self.

Most importantly, regardless of what happened in the past, you have the power to create new paths.

Be cautious, but watch out for new possibilities.

Be unconventional, but tread the world gently.

> We do not live in a perfect world, but you can find your place in it. Hold your head high, and be at peace.
>
> When it comes to finding your place in the world, wish not for an 'easy' path, but one that is rich, stimulating, fulfilling, and on which you feel vividly alive.

Journaling exercise: rewind your day

Through this exercise, you can practise becoming an astute observer of both your mental states and your behaviours at work.

At the end of a workday, when you get home in the evening, take about 10 to 15 minutes for a meditative reflection.

Start by closing your eyes and take in three deep breaths.

Now, imagine stepping outside of your body and look back at yourself where you are sitting.

With interest and compassion, notice your posture, the clothes you are wearing, and the look on your face.

Then, in your mind's eye, rewind the day and your actions. Start from the chair you are sitting on, think back to your journey home, then to the moment you left the office, and go back into your workspace. Go back scene by scene, moment by moment, until you reach the beginning of your working day.

Try to recall as many details as possible and watch yourself with curiosity and patience. When emotions arise, see if you can remain in the position of an observer, as though you are watching your thoughts and feelings play out on a television screen.

Imagine that you were just an actor in a show, and that all those around you were characters in the same drama.

Carry out the above exercise for five consecutive days. During this process, reflect on the following questions, and write your answers in a journal.

1 Be mindful of moments where you felt vulnerable, anxious or humiliated.
   - Was this because you lost external validation?
   - What kind of recognition were you seeking? For example, were you wanting praise for your competence or your appearance, or the reassurance that you were doing well?
   - What age do you feel on the inside when you are waiting for validation from another person?
   - How do you tend to react to situations where you feel helpless, humiliated or ashamed?

2 Take note of times where you feel irritated, impatient or judgemental towards others. Think of these as mild forms of anger. By noticing and accepting the seeds of anger when they first arise, you can stop them from escalating.
   - Ask yourself: what kind of issues tend to create tension in you?

- Tune in to your body. Where in your body do you feel tensions?
- Do you usually turn anger outward, or inward? Do you binge eat, drink, or numb out after an episode of anger?
- Are you afraid of getting out of control at work? How long does it take for your anger to pass?

3 Now, list some moments when you did something you were proud of. It doesn't have to be something substantial, but may be things like taking the time to talk to a stranger or helping someone out.
- What values or virtues do they reflect? (For example, respect, loyalty, kindness.)
- What kind of opportunities would allow you to become more like the person you want to be?

4 Imagine a world in which you can live without fears, and be the person you want to be. In this new reality, you will go into work embodying the values that you want to manifest in the world (for example, integrity, authenticity, respect).
- How would you look, walk and talk differently?
- How would you relate to those around you?
- When conflict arises, what stance would you take?
- When you are unfairly accused or oppressed, how might you react differently?
- How would you talk to yourself differently?
- What might you start doing?
- What would you stop doing?
- What hopes, dreams and visions may emerge from this new way of being?
- What changes would other people notice?

Now, identify one small change that you can make in order to be more like the person you want to be.

Growing out of people

Do you hold on to people and places that no longer serve you?

Does it pain you a great deal to see that some relationships have changed shape and are no longer what they once were?

Do you deny the fact that you have become more successful than your old friends and family could ever comprehend?

By nature, intense people are fast-moving. Personal and spiritual growth comes to you at lightning speed, and your life is one adventure after another. When you are stagnant, you battle with boredom, irritation and an unbearable sense of unfulfillment. When you overstay in a relationship or friendship, your truth screams at you. It may start with small irritations but soon fester into chronic dissatisfaction and resentment. With a broad mind, open heart, and hunger for growth, you have difficulty finding companions to meet you at your intellectual, emotional and spiritual depth. In the search for connections, you have to find kinship from cultures and people from across time and space.

Being a non-conformist, you have a natural desire to break away from the limited worldviews and social confines that were imposed upon you. Walking away from the herd mentality is not just a longing, but a calling, and it is the only thing you can do. Your innate drive takes you to places far beyond what people in your old world could comprehend. Whenever you go back to where you have come from, however, you may find yourself more alienated than ever before. You realize, though not without pain, that you no longer have anything in common with your old friends. As you move to the next place, this pattern replicates itself. One day, you realize that outgrowing people, places and community has become 'the story of your life'.

The inevitable change

Whenever you grow into the next level of consciousness, some people in your life may have a hard time keeping up with the change. With the retrieval of your true self, you begin to say what you mean, and express how you feel. Instead of playing small, you reclaim your creative space and allow your intensity to be seen. The new you emits a vibration that is too dazzling for those who are not ready. Even when you do not intend to, you become a threat to those who live in the 'old world' of conventional wisdom and the false security of tradition. Your existence represents their secret desires. In all terror and glory they too, deep down, yearn to be liberated. But they are not ready to question the only authorities they know, shake up the security they have, question the only relationships they rely on, or risk growing into the unknown. Your move lures their inner rebel to scratch a soul itch, and to avoid their unbearable inner conflicts they have to undermine your path in order to validate theirs.

People by and large feel comfortable within the existing equilibrium of a relationship dynamic. When you expand your sense of self, something shifts. Your old friends will have to adjust not just to the new you, but also their new selves – the selves they will have to be when they are with you. If they are not growing alongside you, it is inevitable that the relationship will become stale, dysfunctional, and even hurtful. Some people, for example, cannot face their own vulnerabilities and tend to project weakness externally; they only know how to be the 'rescuer' in a relationship. As you become less dependent on them, they may feel abandoned or rejected by you. If they are no longer the helper, or the one in charge, who are they now? This question may be too uncomfortable for them to face. So they continue to relate to you in the old ways, hoping to resume the old dysfunctional dynamic that had kept you needy and dependent.

Without careful examination, you may not notice the very subtle ways your old friends undermine you. For example, instead of asking what is going well, they play the devil's advocate. They suggest you are moving too fast, or warn against future disappointment. They show excessive concern for your health or talk to you in infantilizing, patronizing ways. If what they say plays into your insecurities, you may then respond unconsciously to take care of their needs. Eerily, you find yourself seeking reassurance when you don't need to, and asking for advice when you don't need it. You play up your worries and hide good news. It is as though you regress to take care of their need for you to stay as the person they knew. On the surface, they are caring for you, but you find yourself walking away from a supposedly friendly interaction with decreased strengths and confidence.

You never intend to invalidate other people's life choices. When you grow or move away, you are running for your life, doing the only thing you know will quench the existential thirst. However, whenever you rebel against the old, disobey your parents' prescribed plan, or go against society's dogma, you face push-backs from multiple directions. You are told – in words, unwelcome gaze and unvoiced pressure – that you are selfish, disrespectful, arrogant. Internalized toxic guilt becomes anxiety and self-doubt. As a result, you may now wonder if you really are a judgemental and arrogant person; you worry you are betraying those who love you. You also fear the loneliness in choosing the path less travelled. You ask: where is my home? Do I have a tribe? Will I ever belong anywhere?

The pain of shedding

Even if their words or actions undermine you, it does not mean your friends and family do not love you. Most of the time, what they say or do are not malicious attacks, but a fight-or-flight response to a perceived threat to their belief system. When you bloom into something beyond their comprehension, bringing you down may be the only way they know to protect the equilibrium of their psyche. They may want the best for you, but their fears limit their capacity to be wholeheartedly supportive of you.

Noticing this pattern does not mean you need to end a relationship or friendship. In order to prevent this dynamic disempowering you, it may be enough to simply become aware of what is happening. Once you see the deeper layer of what is going on, you can work towards becoming unperturbed by their projections. If necessary, you can manage your expectations and what you intend to give and take from the relationship, and become the bigger person who holds their friend's vulnerabilities in compassion.

Sometimes, however, the only way forward is to move on from a relationship. No matter how much someone or something was important to you in the past, it may no longer have the same place in your new life. As a sensitive person, you are sensitized to the hypocrisies of pretending something remains the same after it has changed. On some level, the other person also realizes the relationship has reached its natural end. If they are not assertive enough to take action, they can resort to passive-aggressive behaviours that are geared to push you away. Sometimes, taking the plunge to break up with a childhood friend, family or a partner is not just safe, but the most loving thing to do.

One of the most delicate balancing acts of human relationships is to honour what you had, and simultaneously release what no longer belongs. We must empty our cups for them to be filled. Holding on to what no longer serves you creates stagnation, resentment and depression.

A break-up does not mean anyone is at fault. You have both done the best you could, based on who you were and what you knew. People come into your life for either a reason, a season, or a lifetime. But no one is meant to stay for a moment too long, beyond the point where it is no longer good for either of you. It is meaningful enough that you had shared laughter, a sorrow, a journey. Nothing is a mistake. Your old relationships are cornerstones in your journey of becoming, and they have brought you to this pivotal point. The way to honour those who have travelled with you is not to hold on, but to let go when the time is ripe.

Grieving and releasing is painful, but this shedding pain is also a growing pain. You are ridding yourself of the tethers so you can fly to answer your calling. Much like the caterpillar that needs to shed her cocoon, you are breaking into something bigger and more glorious. Once you are free to manifest the gifts as an intense person, everyone, including your future self, will thank you. Even when it hurts, see if you can tenderly embrace the pain of saying goodbye and affirm to yourself that the tears are a sign that things are heading in the right direction.

As you make changes to align your surroundings with your new-found identity as a dignified person, inner calm and clarity will emerge. One day, you will realize how free you feel, and that you no longer crave approval from your parents, old friends, or the mainstream world. You will know who you are and feel grounded. It is a wondrous feeling to be able to stretch out your limbs, take up the space that is yours, and to authentically let your vibe attract your tribe.

Ritual: discerning and releasing

You can harness the skill of discerning in order to evaluate if someone has a place in your new life. Start by becoming aware of how you feel – viscerally, emotionally, spiritually – in an interaction with them. Using the following questions, reflect on a particular exchange that you've had:

1 Does the conversation feel natural, easy or forced? Do you have to 'find things to talk about'?

2 Do you feel emotionally connected, or intellectually challenged? Or are you bored and restless?

3 Does it feel safe to share intimate details of your life with them? Do you restrain yourself from sharing good news or play down the positive aspects of your life?

4 Do you feel safe enough to be your full self with them? Or do you feel the need to edit yourself, so you don't come across as being 'too much', 'too emotional', 'too intense'?

5 Do your life goals, values and lifestyles differ greatly? While shared goals and values aren't always essential in friendships, it can be a problem if this means your conversation must remain shallow or if your friend's actions violate the principles of your ethics. Perhaps you feel judgemental towards them but then feel guilty afterwards, and end up in a tiring cycle of emotions.

6 Do you feel guilty and dishonest every time you walk away from an interaction?

7 Are they interested in personal growth or spiritual development? Are they able to reflect on themselves?

8 Is the past the only thing you have in common?

9 Imagine wiping out history. If this were a new person that you have only just met, would you want them in your inner circle?

10 Do you walk away feeling drained, diminished, flat or energized?

11 Does your friendship begin to feel like a chore? Do you look forward to the next meeting, or would you rather be doing something else?

12 Do you feel they passively push you away, for instance by being apathetic or uninterested? Do they appear as though they do not want to be here but do not want to say it?

You may have identified some relationships in your life that you wish to let go of. If it feels right to do so, follow through with a ritual of releasing:

- Prepare a few pieces of paper in different colours.
- Draw or write on each of them people that no longer have a place in your life, or that you would like to release. You can include not only people but a way of relating to them, such as co-dependency.
- Reflect on what makes you hold on to them, and write that on the flip side of the paper.
- Prepare your mind to release them, and imagine what life would be like without them.
- To release, you may burn, rip, or bury these papers. Pay attention to your body and your breathing during the process.
- Set an intention to honour the connection you have with these people/relationships/thoughts, and then let them go.
- Congratulate yourself for allowing yourself to move towards freedom and lightness.

This is a symbolic exercise that aims to create subtle psychological shifts. While the act of burning or tearing things seems brutal, it does not mean you need to do anything drastic in real life. The shift may come in subtle form, such as an increase in assertiveness, a way of thinking about the relationship, or a change in your expectations.

Be assured that with or without your conscious willpower, when the timing is right, what no longer serves you will drop away. In your mind's eye, imagine yourself like a tree in nature.

You do not have to do anything, control anything, or decide on anything. As the season changes, nature will help you shed dead leaves and branches. You will not have to worry about the shape and form of your new fruits either, for you will be provided with the necessary nutrients and resources for the very fruits you are destined to bear.

The invitation to soar

Dear Intense Ones,

Perhaps at some point in your life, you have learned that to be safe you have to shrink and hide.

People in your life have condemned you for saying too much, asking too much, feeling too much.

You were told by the authorities and institutions to be still and to be quiet.

You were socially pressured to not disturb anything, or to not outshine anyone.

You have been threatened by your competitive siblings, and your playfulness and vitality were blunted.

Others may have discharged or projected their psychic shadows onto you, accusing you of the negative traits that they denied in themselves.

Perhaps your family has assigned to you a 'sick role', making you the carrier of all that is grieved.

You were so burdened by having to be the little grown-up, the confidant, the counsellor of everyone around you, that you have forgotten how to play, to be, or to express yourself spontaneously.

You may have stifled your feelings, blunted your ambitions and silenced your voice.

You may have held yourself back with self-sabotage, intense self-criticism or imposter syndrome – the feeling that you are a fraud despite worldly recognition.

Even as you have physically and geographically moved out of your child-hood environment, you continued to live in a cage that you have created in your mind.

But no matter what happened when you were younger, your intense soul remains wild and untamed. It might have been hidden away, but it has not gone away. Regardless of how much you or those around you have tried to shut it down, manipulate it or pretend that it doesn't exist, your passionate soul always breaks through.

It is now time to wake up to a new reality.

Your intensity is not a defect or an illness.

Quite the opposite, being intense means you are endowed with unique qualities that others do not share. Even though it may not provide you with an easy path through life, it is what makes you a great empathizer, artist and visionary. Your idiosyncrasies are not only related to the fact you are gifted; they are gifts in themselves. Now it is up to you to unveil the years of oppression, to stand up straight, and to serve the world with your fullest potential.

As you emerge into your new reality, you no longer have to play small in order to be safe.

Look around you – look carefully and lucidly at your current reality.

The false authorities of your past no longer have power over you.

You are free from the tyranny of toxic envy or competition.

You are no longer haunted by the threat of abandonment or rejection.

You no longer have to play your allocated black sheep role.

You no longer need to use false humility, self-denigration, inner criticism or self-sabotage to protect yourself from your light.

The world is ready to celebrate your beauty, your success, your glory.

Honour the tremendous resilience you have built through life experiences.

Feel how firmly your feet are rooted to the ground.

No matter what has happened in the past, you now have the power and freedom to reclaim your life.

If anyone passive-aggressively attacks you, gaslights you or manipulates the situation, you will see through it right away.

When someone puts you down or spreads rumours about you, you can trust your integrity to shine through the smokescreen.

Should anyone ask, 'Who do you think you are?' you can reply, 'A humble soul who dares to be real.'

That intense one inside of you is longing to, at long last, be heard, seen and embraced for who they are.

Soar.

References

2: Being intense is a brain difference

1 Brazelton, T.B., Nugent, J. K., & Lester, B.M., Neonatal Behavioral Assessment Scale. In Osofsky, J.D., ed., Wiley series on personality processes, *Handbook of Infant Development* (John Wiley & Sons, 1987), 780–817.

2 Kagan, J., Arcus, D., Snidman, N., Feng, W.Y., Hendler, J. and Greene, S., 'Reactivity in infants: A cross-national comparison', *Developmental Psychology*, 30(3) (1994): 342.

3 Aron, E., *The Highly Sensitive Person* (Kensington Publishing Corp, 2013).

4 Aron, E., *The Highly Sensitive Person*. Available at: https://hsperson.com/ (retrieved 27 December 2019).

5 Aron, E., *The Highly Sensitive Person* (Kensington Publishing Corp, 2013).

6 Csikszentmihalyi, M., *Finding Flow: The Psychology of Engagement with Everyday Life* (Hachette UK, 2020).

7 Boyce, W.T., *The Orchid and the Dandelion: Why Sensitive People Struggle and How All Can Thrive* (Pan Macmillan, 2019).

8 Dobbs, D., *Dandelion Kids and Orchid Children: How vulnerability is responsiveness, danger opportunity, and an apparent weakness – genetically conferred sensitivity to environment – may be the secret to human (and humankind's) success* (Atlantic, 2009).

9 Orloff, J., *The Empath's Survival Guide: Life Strategies for Sensitive People* (Sounds True, 2017).

10 Hatfield, E., Cacioppo, J.T. and Rapson, R.L., 'Emotional contagion', *Studies in Emotion and Social Interaction* (Cambridge University Press, 1994).

11 Hatfield, E., Cacioppo, J.T. and Rapson, R.L., 'Emotional contagion', *Studies in Emotion and Social Interaction* (Cambridge University Press, 1994).

12 Hatfield, E., Cacioppo, J.T. and Rapson, R.L., 'Emotional contagion', *Studies in Emotion and Social Interaction* (Cambridge University Press, 1994).

13 Decety, J. and Lamm, C., Human empathy through the lens of social neuroscience, *The Scientific World Journal*, 6 (2006): 1146–1163; Decety, J. and Svetlova, M., 'Putting together phylogenetic and ontogenetic perspectives on empathy', *Developmental Cognitive Neuroscience* 2, no. 1 (2012): 1–24; Preston, S.D. and De Waal, F.B., 'Empathy: Its ultimate and proximate bases', *Behavioral and Brain Sciences* 25, no. 1 (2002): 1–20; Prochazkova, E. and Kret, M.E., 'Connecting minds and sharing emotions through mimicry: A neurocognitive model of emotional contagion', *Neuroscience & Biobehavioral Reviews* 80 (2017): 99–114.

14 Gallese, V., 'Mirror neurons and intentional attunement: Commentary on Olds', *Journal of the American Psychoanalytic Association* 54, no. 1 (2006): 47–57; Gallese, V. and Goldman, A., 'Mirror neurons and the simulation theory of mind-reading', *Trends in Cognitive Sciences* 2, no. 12 (1998): 493–501; Keysers, C. and Gazzola, V., 'Social neuroscience: mirror neurons recorded in humans', *Current Biology* 20, no. 8 (2010): R353–R354.

15 Jackson, A.W., Horinek, D.F., Boyd, M.R. and McClellan, A.D., 'Disruption of left–right reciprocal coupling in the spinal cord of larval lamprey abolishes brain-initiated locomotor activity', *Journal of Neurophysiology* 94, no. 3 (2005): 2031–2044; Lloyd, D., Di Pellegrino, G. and Roberts, N., 'Vicarious

responses to pain in anterior cingulate cortex: is empathy a multisensory issue?' *Cognitive, Affective, & Behavioral Neuroscience* 4, no. 2 (2004): 270–278; Prehn-Kristensen, A., Wiesner, C., Bergmann, T.O., Wolff, S., Jansen, O., Mehdorn, H.M., … and Pause, B.M., 'Induction of empathy by the smell of anxiety', *PLoS ONE* 4, no. 6 (2009): e5987.

16 De Vignemont, F. and Singer, T., 'The empathic brain: How, when and why?' *Trends in Cognitive Sciences* 10, no. 10 (2006): 435–441.

17 Adolphs, R., Sears, L. and Piven, J., 'Abnormal processing of social information from faces in autism', *Journal of Cognitive Neuroscience* 13, no. 2 (2001): 232–240.

18 Heylighen, F., *Gifted People and Their Problems*, (Davidson Institute for Talent Development, 2012), 1–2; Lind, S., 'Overexcitability and the gifted' *The SENG Newsletter* 1, no. 1 (2001): 3–6; Tucker, B., Hafenstein, .L., Jones, S., Bernick, R. and Haines, K., 'An integrated-thematic curriculum for gifted learners', *Roeper Review* 19, no. 4 (1997): 196–199.

19 Gardner, H.E., *Intelligence Reframed: Multiple Intelligences for the 21st Century* (Hachette UK, 2000).

20 Karpinski, R.I., Kolb, A.M.K., Tetreault, N.A. and Borowski, T.B., 'High intelligence: A risk factor for psychological and physiological overexcitabilities', *Intelligence* 66 (2018): 8–23.

21 Dąbrowski, Kazimierz, M.D, *Positive Disintegration* (J. & A. Churchill Ltd, 1964).

22 The following descriptions are drawn from: Piechowski, M. M. *Overexcitabilities*. Retrieved April 28, 2020, from https://www.positivedisintegration.com/Piechowski1999.pdf; Webb, J.T., Amend, E.R., Webb, N.E., Goerss, J., Beljan, P. and Olenchak, F.R., *Misdiagnosis and Dual Diagnosis of Gifted Children and Adults: ADHD, Bipolar, OCD, Asperger's Depression, and Other Disorders* (Great Potential Press, Inc., 2005).

23 Siaud-Facchin, J., *L'enfant surdoué* (Odile Jacob, 2012).

24 Karpinski, R.I., Kolb, A.M.K., Tetreault, N.A. and Borowski, T.B., 'High intelligence: A risk factor for psychological and physiological overexcitabilities', *Intelligence* 66 (2018): 8–23.

25 Saltz, G., *The Power of Different: The Link Between Disorder and Genius* (Macmillan, 2017).

26 Pulcu, E., Zahn, R., Moll, J., Trotter, P.D., Thomas, E.J., Juhasz, G., ... and Elliott, R., 'Enhanced subgenual cingulate response to altruistic decisions in remitted major depressive disorder', *NeuroImage: Clinical* 4 (2014): 701–710.

27 Bradley, B.P., Mogg, K., White, J., Groom, C. and De Bono, J., 'Attentional bias for emotional faces in generalized anxiety disorder', *British Journal of Clinical Psychology* 38, no. 3 (1999): 267–278.

28 Cytowic, R.E., *Synesthesia: A Union of the Senses* (MIT Press, 2002); Geake, J., 'Neural interconnectivity and intellectual creativity: Giftedness, savants and learning styles', *The Routledge International Companion to Gifted Education* (Routledge, 2013), 34–41.

29 Seubert, R., 'P-528 Treating depressive crises more effectively by taking into account overexcitabilities and the 'third factor', *European Psychiatry* 27, no. 1 (2012).

30 Dąbrowski, K., Kawczak, A., and Piechowski, M. N., *Mental Growth Through Positive Disintegration* (Gryf Publications, 1970).

31 Webb, J.T., Amend, E.R., Webb, N.E., Goerss, J., Beljan, P. and Olenchak, F.R., *Misdiagnosis and Dual Diagnosis of Gifted Children and Adults: ADHD, Bipolar, OCD, Asperger's Depression, and Other Disorders* (Great Potential Press, Inc., 2005).

32 Dąbrowski, K, *Psychoneurosis Is Not an Illness: Neuroses and Psychoneuroses from the Perspective of Positive Disintegration* (Gryf Publications, 1972).

33 Storr, A., *Feet of Clay* (Simon and Schuster, 1997), xi.

34 Storr, A., *Feet of Clay* (Simon and Schuster, 1997).

35 Tolle, E., *The Power of Now: A Guide to Spiritual Enlightenment* (New World Library, 2004).

36 Saltz, G., *The Power of Different: The Link Between Disorder and Genius* (Macmillan, 2017).

37 Teigen, K.H., 'Yerkes–Dodson: A law for all seasons', *Theory & Psychology* 4, no. 4 (1994): 525–547.

38 Watts, A. (2016). Available at: https://alanwilsonwatts.tumblr.com/post/148831042676/in-the-spring-scenery-there-is-nothing-superior (retrieved 25 August 2020).

39 Pink, D.H., *A Whole New Mind: Why Right-Brainers Will Rule the Future* (Penguin, 2006).

3: Being out-of-sync with the world

1 McCrae, R.R., 'Openness to experience as a basic dimension of personality', *Imagination, Cognition and Personality* 13, no. 1 (1993): 39–55.

2 Chess, S. and Thomas, A., 'Temperament and the concept of goodness of fit', *Explorations in Temperament* (Springer, 1991), 15–28.

3 Solomon, A., *Far From the Tree: Parents, Children and the Search for Identity* (Simon and Schuster, 2012).

4 Solomon, A., *Far From the Tree: Parents, Children and the Search for Identity* (Simon and Schuster, 2012), 1.

5 Field, T., 'The effects of mother's physical and emotional unavailability on emotion regulation', *Monographs of the Society for Research in Child Development* 59, no. 2 (1994): 208–227; Schore, J.R. and Schore, A.N., 'Modern attachment theory: The central role of affect regulation in development and treatment', *Clinical Social Work Journal* 36, no. 1 (2008): 9–20.

6 Spiegel, A. (2010, November 22) Siblings share genes, but rarely personalities. Available at: https://www.npr.org/2010/11/18/131424595/siblings-share-genes-but-rarely-personalities (retrieved 25 August 2020).

7 Bretherton, I., and Munholland, K. A., *Internal working models in attachment relationships: Elaborating a central construct in attachment theory*. In Cassidy, J. and Shaver, P. R. (Eds.), *Handbook of attachment: Theory, research, and clinical applications* (Guilford Press, 2008), 102–127.

8 Smith, R. H., *Envy and Its Transmutations*. In L. Z. Tiedens & C. Leach, eds., *Studies in emotion and social interaction. The social life of emotions* (Cambridge University Press, 2004), 43–63.

9 Rodriguez Mosquera, P.M., Parrott, W.G. and Hurtado de Mendoza, A., 'I fear your envy, I rejoice in your coveting: On the ambivalent experience of being envied by others', *Journal of Personality and Social Psychology* 99, no. 5 (2010): 842.

10 Duffy, M.K., Scott, K.L., Shaw, J.D., Tepper, B.J. and Aquino, K., 'A social context model of envy and social undermining', *Academy of Management Journal* 55, no. 3 (2012): 643–666.

11 Parrott, W.G., 'The Benefits and Threats from Being Envied in Organizations', 455-474. In Smith, R.H., Merlone, U. and Duffy, M.K., eds., *Envy at Work and in Organizations* (Oxford University Press, 2016).

12 Foster, G.M., 'The anatomy of envy: A study in symbolic behavior', *Current Anthropology* 13 (1972): 165–202.

13 Smith, R.H., Merlone, U. and Duffy, M.K., eds., *Envy at Work and in Organizations* (Oxford University Press, 2016).

14 Monbiot, G., The denial industry, the *Guardian* (2006), 19.

15 Bauman, Z., *Modernity and the Holocaust* (Cornell University Press, 2000).

16 Aronson, E., 'The theory of cognitive dissonance: A current perspective', *Advances in Experimental Social Psychology* 4 (1969):

1–34; John, L.K., Blunden, H. and Liu, H., 'Shooting the messenger', *Journal of Experimental Psychology: General* 148, no. 4 (2019): 644–666, doi.org/10.1037/xge0000586.

17 Wapnick, E. *How to be Everything: A Guide for Those Who (Still) Don't Know what They Want to be When They Grow Up*, (HarperCollins, 2017).

18 Guillebeau, C., *The Art of Non-Conformity: Set Your Own Rules, Live the Life You Want, and Change the World* (Penguin, 2010).

19 Baumeister, R.F. and Leary, M.R., 'The need to belong: Desire for interpersonal attachments as a fundamental human motivation', *Psychological Bulletin* 117, no. 3 (1995): 497.

20 Fiske, S.T., and Yamamoto, M., 'Coping with Rejection: Core social motives across cultures'. In Williams, K.D., Forgas, J.P., and von Hippel, W., eds., Sydney Symposium of Social Psychology series. *The Social Outcast: Ostracism, Social Exclusion, Rejection, and Bullying* (Psychology Press, 2005), 185–198.

21 DeRosier, M.E., Kupersmidt, J.B. and Patterson, C.J., 'Children's academic and behavioral adjustment as a function of the chronicity and proximity of peer rejection', *Child Development* 65, no. 6 (1994): 1799–1813.

22 Renshaw, P.D. and Brown, P.J., 'Loneliness in middle childhood: Concurrent and longitudinal predictors', *Child Development* 64, no. 4 (1993): 1271–1284.

23 Leary, M.R., Cottrell, C.A. and Phillips, M., 'Deconfounding the effects of dominance and social acceptance on self-esteem', *Journal of Personality and Social Psychology* 81, no. 5 (2001): 898.

24 Ladd, G.W. and Troop-Gordon, W., 'The role of chronic peer difficulties in the development of children's psychological adjustment problems', *Child Development* 74, no. 5 (2003): 1344–1367.

25 Gardner, W.L., Pickett, C.L. and Brewer, M.B., 'Social exclusion and selective memory: How the need to belong influences

memory for social events', *Personality and Social Psychology Bulletin* 26, no. 4 (2000): 486–496; Pickett, C.L., Gardner, W.L. and Knowles, M., 'Getting a cue: The need to belong and enhanced sensitivity to social cues', *Personality and Social Psychology Bulletin* 30, no. 9 (2004): 1095–1107; Williams, K.D. and Sommer, K.L., 'Social ostracism by coworkers: Does rejection lead to loafing or compensation?' *Personality and Social Psychology Bulletin* 23, no. 7 (1997): 693–706.

26 Lakin, J.L. and Chartrand, T.L., 'Using nonconscious behavioral mimicry to create affiliation and rapport', *Psychological Science* 14, no. 4 (2003): 334–339; Lakin, J.L., Chartrand, T.L. and Arkin, R.M., 'I am too just like you: Nonconscious mimicry as an automatic behavioral response to social exclusion', *Psychological Science* 19, no. 8 (2008): 816–822.

27 Eisenberger, N.I., 'The neural bases of social pain: evidence for shared representations with physical pain', *Psychosomatic Medicine* 74, no. 2 (2012): 126; Eisenberger, N.I., Jarcho, J.M., Lieberman, M.D. and Naliboff, B.D., 'An experimental study of shared sensitivity to physical pain and social rejection', *Pain* 126, 1–3 (2006): 132–138.

28 Rushen, J., Boissy, A., Terlouw, E.M.C. and de Passillé, A.M.B., 'Opioid peptides and behavioral and physiological responses of dairy cows to social isolation in unfamiliar surroundings', *Journal of Animal Science* 77, no. 11 (1999): 2918–2924.

29 DeWall, C.N. and Baumeister, R.F., 'Alone but feeling no pain: Effects of social exclusion on physical pain tolerance and pain threshold, affective forecasting, and interpersonal empathy', *Journal of Personality and Social Psychology* 91, no. 1 (2006): 1.

30 Twenge, J.M., Catanese, K.R. and Baumeister, R.F., 'Social exclusion and the deconstructed state: Time perception, meaninglessness, lethargy, lack of emotion, and self-awareness', *Journal of Personality and Social Psychology* 85, no. 3 (2003): 409.

4: The relationship with yourself

1 Winnicott, D.W., 'The theory of the parent–infant relationship', *International Journal of Psycho-Analysis* 41 (1960): 585–595.

2 Jung, C.G., *The Collected Works of Carl Jung* (Pantheon, 1953).

3 Jung, C.G., 'The Aims of Psychotherapy', *Collected Works*, vol. 16 (Princeton University Press, 1931): 36–52.

4 Saint John of the Cross, *Dark Night of the Soul: And Other Great Works* (Bridge Logos Foundation, 2007).

5 Kübler-Ross, E., *On Death and Dying* (Routledge, 2008).

6 Sartre, J.P. (1957) *The Transcendence of the Ego: An Existentialist Theory of Consciousness* (Vol. 114), Macmillan.

7 Campbell, J., *The Hero with a Thousand Faces*, vol. 17 (New World Library, 2008).

8 Hesse, H., *Demian* (Courier Corporation, 2000).

9 Harris, R., *ACT Made Simple: An easy-to-read primer on acceptance and commitment therapy* (New Harbinger Publications, 2019); Hayes, S.C., Strosahl, K.D. and Wilson, K.G., *Acceptance and Commitment Therapy: The Process and Practice of Mindful Change* (Guilford Press, 2011).

10 Taylor, J.B., *My Stroke of Insight* (Hachette UK, 2009).

11 Jazaieri, H., McGonigal, K., Jinpa, T., Doty, J.R., Gross, J.J. and Goldin, P.R., 'A randomized controlled trial of compassion cultivation training: Effects on mindfulness, affect, and emotion regulation', *Motivation and Emotion* 38, no. 1 (2014): 23–35.

5: Your relationship with your family

1 Miller, A., *The Drama of the Gifted Child: The Search for the True Self* (Basic Books, 2008).

2 Bowlby, J., *Attachment* (Basic Books, 2008).

3 Niven, K., Totterdell, P. and Holman, D., 'A classification of controlled interpersonal affect regulation strategies', *Emotion* 9, no. 4 (2009): 498.

4 Vangelisti, A.L., 'Family secrets: Forms, functions and correlates', *Journal of Social and Personal Relationships* 11, no. 1 (1994): 113–135.

5 Bowlby, J., *Attachment* (Basic Books, 2008); Field, T., 'The effects of mothers' physical and emotional unavailability on emotion regulation', *Monographs of the Society for Research in Child Development* 59 (1994): 208–227.

6 Zaki, J. and Williams, W.C., 'Interpersonal emotion regulation', *Emotion* 13, no. 5 (2013): 803.

7 Minnick, C., 'Splitting-and-Projective Identification', 2019. Available at: http://minnickskleinacademy.com/module-2-2-kleins-baby-core-coping-defensive-maneuvers/splitting-and-projective-identification/ (retrieved 1 February 2020).

8 Ogden, T.H., 'On projective identification', *The International Journal of Psychoanalysis* 60 (1979): 357–373.

9 Mahler, M.S., Pine, F. and Bergman, A., *The Psychological Birth of the Human Infant. Symbiosis and Individuation* (Basic Books, 1975).

10 Firestone, R.W. and Catlett, J., *Fear of Intimacy* (American Psychological Association, 1999).

11 Mahler, M.S., Pine, F. and Bergman, A., *The Psychological Birth of the Human Infant. Symbiosis and Individuation* (Basic Books, 1975).

12 Brady, M.T., 'Invisibility and insubstantiality in an anorexic adolescent: Phenomenology and dynamics', *Journal of Child Psychotherapy* 37, no. 1 (2011): 3–15.

13 Knafo, D., ed., *Living With Terror, Working With Trauma: A Clinician's Handbook* (Jason Aronson, 2004).

14 Chase, N.D., ed., *Burdened Children: Theory, Research, and Treatment of Parentification* (Sage, 1999).

15 Firestone, R.W. and Catlett, J., *Fear of Intimacy* (American Psychological Association, 1999); Rohner, R.P., 'The parental 'acceptance-rejection syndrome': universal correlates of perceived rejection', *American Psychologist* 59, no. 8 (2004): 830.

16 Flax, J., 'The conflict between nurturance and autonomy in mother-daughter relationships and within feminism', *Feminist Studies* 4, no. 2 (1978): 171–189.

17 Solomon, A., *Far From the Tree: Parents, Children and the Search for Identity* (Simon and Schuster, 2012).

18 Minuchin, S., Baker, L., Rosman, B.L., Liebman, R., Milman, L. and Todd, T.C., 'A conceptual model of psychosomatic illness in children: Family organisation and family therapy', *Archives of General Psychiatry* 32, no. 8 (1975): 1031–1038.

19 Peterson, R. and Green, S., *Families First: Keys to Successful Family Functioning: Family Roles* (Virginia Polytechnic Institute and State University, 2009).

20 Miller, A., *The Body Never Lies: The Lingering Effects of Cruel Parenting* (WW Norton & Company, 2006); Van der Kolk, B.A., *The Body Keeps the Score: Brain, Mind, and Body in the Healing of Trauma* (Penguin Books, 2015).

21 Kalsched, D., *Trauma and the Soul: A Psycho-Spiritual Approach to Human Development and its Interruption* (Routledge/Taylor & Francis Group, 2013).

22 Holmes, E.A., Arntz, A. and Smucker, M.R., 'Imagery rescripting in cognitive behaviour therapy: Images, treatment techniques and outcomes', *Journal of Behavior Therapy and Experimental Psychiatry* 38, no. 4 (2007): 297–305.

23 Geiser, F., Imbierowicz, K., Conrad, R., Wegener, I. and Liedtke, R., 'Turning against self and its relation to symptom distress, interpersonal problems, and therapy outcome: A

replicated and enhanced study', *Psychotherapy Research* 15, no. 4 (2005): 357–365; Geiser, F., Schulz-Werner, A., Imbierowicz, K., Conrad, R. and Liedtke, R., 'Impact of the turning-against-self defense mechanism on the process and outcome of inpatient psychotherapy', *Psychotherapy Research* 13, no. 3 (2003): 355–370.

24 Fairbairn, W.R.D., *Psychoanalytic Studies of the Personality* (Routledge, 1952).

25 Luke, H.M., *Dark Wood to White Rose: A Study of Meanings in Dante's Divine Comedy* (Dove Publications, 1975), 39.

26 Gibran, K., 'On Children', 1923, n.d.. Available at: https://poets.org/poem/children-1 (retrieved 13 February 2020)

6: Romantic and intimate relationships

1 Ellison, N., Heino, R. and Gibbs, J., 'Managing impressions online: Self-presentation processes in the online dating environment', *Journal of Computer-Mediated Communication* 11, no. 2 (2006): 415–441; Toma, C.L., Hancock, J.T. and Ellison, N.B., 'Separating fact from fiction: An examination of deceptive self-presentation in online dating profiles', *Personality and Social Psychology Bulletin* 34, no. 8 (2008): 1023–1036.

2 Hatfield, E., and Walster, G.W., *A New Look at Love* (University Press of America, 1985); Hatfield, E. and Sprecher, S., 'The passionate love scale'. In *Handbook of Sexuality-Related Measures,* 3rd ed. (Routledge, 2010), 469–472.

3 Wachtel, E.F., *The Heart of Couple Therapy: Knowing What To Do and How To Do It* (Guilford Publications, 2016).

4 Kroeger, O., *Type Talk, or, How to Determine Your Personality Type and Change Your Life* (Delacorte Press, 1988).

5 Wachtel, E.F., *The Heart of Couple Therapy: Knowing What To Do and How To Do It* (Guilford Publications, 2016).

6 Jacoby, M., *The Analytic Encounter: Transference and Human Relationship* (Inner City Books, 1984).

7 Howe, D. *Child Abuse and Neglect: Attachment, Development and Intervention*, (Macmillan International Higher Education, 2005).

8 Schore, A.N., 'Early shame experiences and infant brain development'. In Gilbert, P. and Andrews, B., eds., *Shame: Interpersonal Behavior, Psychopathology, and Culture* (Oxford University Press, 1998), 57–77.

9 Samplin, E., Ikuta, T., Malhotra, A.K., Szeszko, P.R. and DeRosse, P., 'Sex differences in resilience to childhood maltreatment: Effects of trauma history on hippocampal volume, general cognition and subclinical psychosis in healthy adults', *Journal of Psychiatric Research* 47, no. 9 (2013): 1174–1179.

10 Takiguchi, S., Fujisawa, T.X., Mizushima, S., Saito, D.N., Okamoto, Y., Shimada, K., ... and Hiratani, M., 'Ventral striatum dysfunction in children and adolescents with reactive attachment disorder: Functional MRI study', *BJPsych open* 1, no. 2 (2015): 121–128.

11 Frodl, T., Reinhold, E., Koutsouleris, N., Reiser, M. and Meisenzahl, E.M., 'Interaction of childhood stress with hippocampus and prefrontal cortex volume reduction in major depression', *Journal of Psychiatric Research* 44, no. 13 (2010): 799–807; Sieff, D.F., *Understanding and Healing Emotional Trauma: Conversations with Pioneering Clinicians and Researchers* (Routledge, 2014).

12 Mikulincer, M. and Florian, V., 'The relationship between adult attachment styles and emotional and cognitive reactions to stressful events'. In Simpson, J.A. and Rholes, W.S., eds., *Attachment Theory and Close Relationships* (Guilford Press, 1998), 143–165.

13 George, C. and Main, M., 'Social interactions of young abused children: Approach, avoidance, and aggression', *Child Development* 50 (1979): 306–318.

14 McWilliams, N., *Psychoanalytic Diagnosis: Understanding Personality Structure in the Clinical Process* (Guilford Press, 2011).

7: Work relationships and friendships

1 Celani, D., *The Treatment of the Borderline Patient: Applying Fairbairn's Object Relations Theory in the Clinical Setting* (International Universities Press, 1993).

2 Erlich, H.S., 'Enemies within and without: Paranoia and regression in groups and organizations', *The Systems Psychodynamics of Organizations* (Routledge, 2018), 115–131.

3 Erlich, H.S., 'Enemies within and without: Paranoia and regression in groups and organizations', *The Systems Psychodynamics of Organizations* (Routledge, 2018), 115–131.

4 Obholzer, A., 'Fragmentation and integration in a school for physically handicapped children', *The Unconscious at Work* (Routledge, 2003), 104–113.

Index

About the Author

Imi Lo is a psychotherapist, art therapist, and consultant for emotionally intense and highly sensitive people. She is the author of two books, *Emotional Sensitivity and Intensity* and *The Gift of Intensity*. Imi specialises in emotional intensity, high sensitivity, giftedness, complex trauma (CPTSD), and personality disorders.

Imi is qualified as a psychotherapist, art psychotherapist, schema therapist, philosophical counsellor, mentalisation-based treatment practitioner, supervisor and mindfulness teacher. With more than a decade of experience, she has worked in the NHS, charities, and other mental health settings. Now, as an independent consultant, she works holistically, combining East and Western philosophies with psychological and spiritual-healing modalities.

Imi is the recipient of multiple scholarships and awards, including the Endeavour Award by the Australian Government. She has been consulted and featured in publications such as *Psychologies Magazine*, *The Telegraph*, *Marie Claire*, and the *Daily Mail*.

She founded Eggshell Therapy and Coaching, where she works with intense people from around the world.

www.eggshelltherapy.com